PURE
POWER

PURE POWER

*A Spiritual Workout to Help
You Break Free from Sexual Sin
. . . or Avoid It in the First Place*

NICOLE ABISINIO

TAN Books
Charlotte, North Carolina

Unless otherwise noted, Scripture texts are from THE HOLY BIBLE, NEW INTERNATIONAL VERSION®, NIV® Copyright © 1973, 1978, 1984, 2011 by Biblica, Inc.® Used by permission. All rights reserved worldwide.

Scripture quotations marked NLT are taken from the Holy Bible, New Living Translation, copyright © 1996, 2004, 2015 by Tyndale House Foundation. Used by permission of Tyndale House Publishers, Inc., Carol Stream, Illinois 60188. All rights reserved.

Cover design by Caroline K. Green

Cover image: "Closeup moment of impact on punching bag," photo by nazarovsergey / Shutterstock

Library of Congress Control Number: 2019952319

ISBN: 978-1-5051-1509-3

Published in the United States by
TAN Books
PO Box 410487
Charlotte, NC 28241
www.TANBooks.com

Printed in the United States of America

Train yourself to be godly. For physical training is of some value, but godliness has value for all things, holding promise for both the present life and the life to come.

1 Timothy 4:7–8

CONTENTS

Preface . . . . *ix*

Introduction: God's Artwork of Purity 1

1 Warm-up and Evaluation 3

2 Restocking Your Spiritual Kitchen:
  Renew Your Mind 16

3 Strength Training: Forgiveness 32

4 Stamina Building and Spiritual Sculpting:
  Power of Prayer and Fasting 44

5 Kickboxing Unhealthy Soul Ties and
  Generational Bondages 62

6 Forty-Day Devotional for Purity 66

7 Daily Vitamins: The Church 108

PREFACE

TO find the person God ordained for us, we have to first become the person God intended us to be. To find the dream spouse, we have to become the dream ourselves. The truth is, I am nothing without the Lord Jesus, and I can do nothing without him, but all things with him. I am a branch on his tree. I am here to produce fruit for the Lord and to have life and have it more abundantly. To truly live is to live in the Spirit and die to the flesh, while devoting every day to defeating the darkness by filling up with the light.

God often humbles me by showing me that in a moment, he could send me back to where I came from. To many in the world, my past life would have made it seem like I was living the dream. I was paying Manhattan bills doing what I love in the film industry. I was working with famous people, acting, casting, and producing. I had people doing my hair, makeup, and shopping for my wardrobe, even designing clothes from scratch just for me. I could have had pretty much any man I wanted: handsome, talented, rich, and powerful. I was right where so many people dream to be, and I was completely empty inside.

All those years, I was chasing my dream job, my dream man, my dream life, but none of it got me the happiness I so desperately desired. It took me attaining each and every one of my dreams to teach me that I could count it all as loss. The Lord is and was the only thing that could ever make me truly happy. Without him at the center and the head of it all, none of it meant anything. He is the Alpha and the Omega. Jesus is the way, the truth, and the life.

It is in the most terrifying and the most magnificently loving moments that God reminds me how far I've come and just how deep that pit of emptiness was that he pulled me out of years ago. He shows me that it is only through him, and him alone, that I am full, complete, and free!

I ask that you, through this book and this journey to be made white as snow, please continue to go to God at every turn, every temptation, and every moment. When things get tough, remember, "With man this is impossible, but with God all things are possible" (Mt 19:26). He will carry you to the Promised Land. And boy, is it a wonderful place to live!

I dedicate this book to the three the Lord has given me: my mom, my mentor, and my best friend, as they have covered me in prayer protection through this journey. I also dedicate this to my dear friend Suzanne Phillips, who passed away in an accident one week before I completed this book. I know she will be smiling down. Above all, I thank my spiritual family—the Father, the Son, and the Holy Spirit—for never leaving me and always taking me to new heights.

Introduction

GOD'S ARTWORK OF PURITY

I F you ever moved with your family as a child and started
a new school, you may remember two feelings: one was
a huge question mark of what lay ahead in your future; the
other feeling was the fresh start. It meant you had a chance
to begin again, to be whoever you wanted to be. I remember
dreaming of being better than my former self. A chance to
be happy, to do things different this time, to have new, better relationships, and an overall brand new chance at life.

That's what Jesus offers us with his forgiveness and
mercy. You start here today with a clean slate. Your past
does not define you. And guess what? It doesn't determine
your future either. Thanks to God, once you repent of any
sexual sins of your past, God will begin to give you a brand
new, more abundant life. Now you can move into your new
home and city with a whole new wardrobe. It's going to be
increasingly beautiful and peaceful, and it's more than you
could ever imagine.

If you are thinking, "That's not true. I still have these same
clothes, same cracks in the walls, same stains on the furni-
ture, same list of mistakes. Yeah, I'm just still me, a broken
mess," renounce that mindset, in Jesus's name. Leave that

falsehood behind with your past. You are cloaked in the robes of royalty by the king our God, and he is leading you into the royal family to which you are called.

Always remember Rahab, a lowly prostitute who chose to trust and fear the Lord our God. Not only did God save her life and those of her family for choosing to follow him, she actually became part of Jesus's bloodline. If God will save the life of a prostitute and put her in the bloodline of his only son, what can and will he do for you? The amazing possibilities are endless. You have a chance in this moment for a clean slate and a fresh start. Let's get this journey started! It's going to be the best one of your entire life!

Chapter 1

WARM-UP AND EVALUATION

THROUGHOUT my experience spiritually coaching singles over the past few years, I realized the most comparable analogy is that of exercising the body. When people want to get their physical body in shape, they work out their exteriors. The same goes for chastity and spiritual training overall. If we want to get in shape, we have to work out our insides. I'm sure you realize that if you slack off at the gym, you almost immediately start to notice a difference. "A little extra inch to pinch," we say. When we slack in our spiritual exercises—prayer, fasting, bible study, church, and fellowship—it has the same effect. We start to go backwards, and our insides start to look less attractive very quickly. The longer you slack, the harder it is to get back on track. The next thing you know, you are living in sweatpants on the couch with a bag of chips and a depressed mood.

The great news is, like the body, there is always time to go gangbusters and get that chiseled look of holiness. People see me as much younger now than they did ten years ago, and when they ask my secret, I always say the Holy Spirit is the fountain of youth. Think about it for a moment.

We work out our bodies that only last eighty to one hundred years at most. People spend so much time getting their body in shape at the gym, styling their hair, or shopping for clothes to "look good." But how little time they spend on getting their inner spirit in shape. Working out our spirits (which will last for eternity) seems to be a more logical priority! Also, much like working out at the gym or with sports, it makes you feel younger and more energized. You feel more alive and often come out with a better attitude and a calmer demeanor. When you see people living in the Spirit, they have this amazing glow about them and you can just tell they have a heavenly chiseled spirit under that body. That's what I want for you through these spiritual workout chapters! As Arnie would say with that thick Aussie accent in the SNL spoof with Hans and Franz, "I'm going to pump you up!"

I was coaching a young man recently over the phone. At the end of our session, he said to me, "So by the end of this spiritual work, you're basically saying I'm going to be like a superhero." I truly pondered that idea for a moment, and then I said, "Yes, yes indeed." If you really think about it, Superman can leap tall buildings with a single bound, the Hulk has superhuman strength. Spiderman has the ability to be personally healed from injury much faster than any human. Then compare those powers to those of Jesus. Not only is he the real deal compared to his comic book counterparts, he is also the ultimate powerhouse of a superhero, and, really, nothing and no one else compares. He healed other people of their sickness and freed people from bondage. He overcame death. Jesus says in the Bible, "I will do whatever you ask in my name, so that the Father may be glorified in the Son" (Jn 14:13). When I look at how far the Lord has brought me and how far he has brought every person he has lifted up through me on this journey to chastity, there is no doubting the power of God.

Wherever you start this journey today, if you do the work in this book and you believe that Jesus can and will free you from this bondage, he absolutely will. In the power of the Holy Spirit, we are able to overcome sin and become superheroes in Christ Jesus.

The fact that you are reading this means that you are currently in one of three categories: You are already living chastely and need some extra strengthening to make the journey easier for you. Or you are a virgin but one who is feeling some temptation and you want to make sure you don't fall. Or you are like I was: You aren't practicing chastity right now and may have already stopped some sexual sins but cannot seem to overcome others. You have the heart to change, but you simply have no idea how to succeed.

All of you are in the right place. Now, as your spiritual personal trainer, I want to start off by telling you I'm already proud of you. The fact that you are reading this now and are starting this journey is half the battle. On days when I don't want to go to the gym but I manage to drag myself there no matter how exhausted, lazy, or busy, I always make some positive progress. Even as you are reading this, you are already making progress in your spirit. However, before we jump into some amazing and powerful spiritual workouts, we need to first analyze your starting point on this journey. Many of us today expect major results for minimum work. We've been conditioned to believe so in this infomercial, "Five minutes will get you ripped," society. It's really important to make sure we are willing to put in the hard work it will truly take to win that trophy of purity. What will help with that effort is to have not only our benefits clarified but first our motivation must be clear!

When you begin with a personal trainer for exercise, you first have to take your current status into account. How often have you been working out those muscles? What's your current fat content? How long can you run without hyperventilating? How much weight can you bench-press before it crushes you? In spiritual personal training, there are many questions I ask in the evaluation that you may want to ask yourself. They include: How often are you praying to work out those spiritual muscles? What's your current area of weakness or weaknesses regarding sexual sin? However, the most important question to focus on and discuss is: *Why* do you want to be chaste?

If you are reading this book, you most certainly want to attain chastity, but the reason why is going to be key to your success. Stop reading for a moment and really focus on your true answer. If your reasons for those goals aren't right to begin with, we won't be able to make the progress that you deserve and would otherwise achieve.

LOVING GOD

If your reason for wanting to be chaste is anything other than your pure love for Christ and complete adoration for Father, Son, and Holy Spirit, we have to first change this foundation. A deep love for God is crucial to success on this journey. Just as it is important for maximum results to know how the body works and how to love our bodies enough to want to take care of them, it is similarly important in the spiritual realm to understand how to love God and how much he loves us before starting our spiritual workouts.

God says, "Love the LORD your God with all your heart and with all your soul and with all your strength" (Dt 6:5). We need to love God with everything we are and everything we have. In the garden, "the LORD God formed a man from the dust of the ground and breathed into his nostrils the breath of life, and the man became a living being" (Gn 2:7). We only have breath in our lungs because God breathed that life into us, so that's a great motivation to do things his way.

When people ask me why I'm chaste now and waiting to have sex until marriage, I always say, "Because I don't want to hurt Jesus," or, "The Lord knows what's best for my life, and I trust him completely." Jesus has our best interest at heart. He has already given us the greatest gift there is. He died on the Cross so that we can really live. Jesus promises and reminds us that keeping God's commands allows us to remain in that love. One of those commands is to stay away from all sexual immorality. Being chaste, then, is a major way for us to show God our absolute love for him!

I learned along the journey that anything God asks us to do will help us reach our full potential as a Godly being. Many of you know by now, from making choices not in line with God's commandments, that true fulfillment can only be found following God's ways, whether we fully understand them or not. All you need to start with is the purity of heart that is needed to please God, to love God, and to give yourself only to God and your future spouse.

GOD'S LOVE FOR US

It's also very important as a motivation to understand and remember how much God loves us. We are each very special to the Lord. When we exercise our bodies, we often put up motivational quotes or post pictures of people in perfect shape. With that in mind, I'm going to list some of my favorite quotes from God, reminding us of his love for us to keep you motivated.

"For God so loved the world that he gave his one and only Son, that whoever believes in him shall not perish but have eternal life" (Jn 3:16).

"Before I formed you in the womb, I knew you, before you were born I set you apart" (Jer 1:5).

"And even the very hairs of your head are all numbered" (Mt 10:30).

"I am fearfully and wonderfully made" (Ps 139:14).

"For we are God's handiwork, created in Christ Jesus to do good works, which God prepared in advance for us to do" (Eph 2:10).

Maybe you don't realize how much God loves you. Maybe you feel like you aren't worthy of being loved by God. Look at the apostles. We know how much Jesus loved them. In fact, the very last thing Jesus did before going to the garden of Gethsemane, knowing he was about to be tortured and killed, was to pray for his apostles and ask that they be protected in the world. These same friends fell asleep when they were supposed to stay up and watch to protect Jesus. They ran away and hid for Jesus's crucifixion while only Mary, Christ's mother, John, and Mary of Magdalene were at the foot of the cross at the end. Peter even denied Jesus three times, and still Jesus gave him the keys to the kingdom when Peter came back and declared his full love and commitment to him. In fact, he welcomed all those disciples back into his loving arms. God says that nothing can separate us from his love. God cannot break his promises. Right now, he welcomes you too back into his loving arms. Choose to embrace him and be loved by him.

If you already have the right motivations, then your "spirit is willing, but the flesh is weak" (Mt 26:41). If you want, with all your heart, to be whom Christ wants you to be, then what a beautiful place to start. The disciples failed during that time in the garden of Gethsemane, but they certainly rose to their God-given ability and overcame once Jesus was raised from the dead and were led to new heights of spiritual strength once the Holy Spirit was given to them after Jesus ascended.

If you realize from reading this that you have any other reason for chastity till marriage, it's important to be aware so you can first change your motivation. Sometimes people start to work out at the gym but don't finish the journey because their initial intention could not carry them through. It's usually "my spouse wants me to get in shape." "My doctor says I need to work out." Your reason for spiritually working out for chastity needs to be strong enough to overcome both flesh and principalities. Remember, Paul says, "For our struggle is not against flesh and blood, but against the rulers, against the authorities, against the powers of this dark world" (Eph 6:12). That's going to take very strong and focused love between you and God to defeat those kinds of enemies. While reasons such as "well the Bible tells me to do it," or, "I've been hurt and I don't want to be hurt again," are both true, it is always higher or better if we do what we do out of love.

That being said, through this journey, you'll find that the more you live a Christlike life, the more you will be rewarded, as long as the reason is to seek God and his kingdom first. Here are some of the amazing benefits coming your way on this journey.

You give God and yourself the opportunity to bring the

right partner and allow a potential future spouse to treat you as *the treasure you are!*

I'm sure you have heard before people can only disrespect you to the extent you allow them. The more you present yourself as a holy child of God, the more others will treat you as such and the more a potential partner will seriously consider if you two are to be married. It makes your potential mate really look at who you are in your spirit instead of all the worldly bells and whistles, and, thus, more readily consider important questions for marriage. Am I called and ready for married life? Is this the person I am going to dedicate myself to for a life together? Are we equally yoked?

In the first week of a recent relationship, the courting process was underway. Instead of wanting to know what my favorite color or movie was, he was asking me serious, important questions to see if we matched up on important life matters. This included children, lifestyle, even where we would be married. We even would play fun games with it such as "fun facts" about ourselves. It avoids a heartbreak to speak early on about crucial issues that can make or break a relationship. He was also very respectful of my love for God, and because I was strong in chastity, even though he had not been chaste himself prior to us courting, he fully respected me at all times and became chaste himself. When we invite the Holy Spirit to put a guard on our hearts and bodies, he protects and convicts others' hearts, no matter where others are in their journey. Hopefully, they will respond to that grace.

God wants his best for us, and it's important for us to constantly remind ourselves to *also* want God's best for us. So even if there is the love with someone, you may not be God's best for each other. He knows those things, and through following his word, neither you nor your potential spouse will end up with someone not ordained by God.

There is nothing wrong with wanting a matching sock. If you are like me in the morning sock hunt, you can be ill prepared. Then you find yourself running around in a hurry and end up grabbing a sock that doesn't match as you run out the door. You can somewhat get away with it if they are both similar in certain ways, but if you look closely, it's weird, it doesn't match, and something is just off. That's how it is and will be with most potential partners. They are not God's best for you. Can you get away with it? If you don't look too closely, if you hide the mismatched parts, but why not wait to find your matching sock? That person may be hiding. Your life partner may be in a different load of laundry while being prepared for you or vice versa. Maybe the one God has ordained for you still needs to be cleaned, or still needs to be dried out! But like missing socks, that person will turn up when you least expect it. And until that happens, wear shoes without socks. Don't go running around with mismatched ones and look like a fool! In other words, don't date just to date.

RECEIVE YOUR SUPERHERO POWERS!

This is my favorite benefit of all. Like the Spiderman quote that actually originates its theme from the Bible, "With great power, comes great responsibility," the more you go in the direction of following God's ways, and knock out this major area of sin, the more your spiritual gifts will start to come out and the more the Lord will use you in mighty ways. Again, while we can't make this benefit our chief motivation to live a holy life for God, it's still a beautiful blessing we receive, using it to further love and serve the Lord. As Paul says, "He gives one person the power to perform miracles, and another the ability to prophesy. He gives someone else the ability to discern whether a message is from the Spirit of God or from another spirit. Still another person is given the ability to speak in unknown languages, while another is given the ability to interpret what is being said" (1 Cor 12:10 NLT).

This is why when you start to make progress in chastity, the enemy tries even harder to trip you up and to set you back. Be on guard. Remember, Satan's job is to steal, kill, and destroy. That means he wants to rob you of God's promises for your life. "He has created us anew in Christ Jesus, so we can do the good things he planned for us long ago" (Eph 2:10 NLT). Chastity is one of these important renewals. If Satan can keep you in bondage through sin, he can rob you of your inheritance, as sin blocks us from God's gifts. It's like putting a wall between you and Jesus.

On the other side of that wall, which is freedom from

sexual sin, is found also Jesus's free flowing of blessings. God loves you either way. He has grace, mercy, and endless love for you. But we have to stop blocking him from giving a lot of those gifts. Each of us was born for a very wonderful and specific purpose for God. That cannot come to fruition until we unblock those blessings. How amazing it is when you are able to receive fully God's plan and purpose for your life.

GAIN YOUR LIFE LIKE NEVER BEFORE!

Following God's ways in our thoughts and actions brings greater joy, peace, and health to you and your relationship. When you are aligned with God's will, the blessings of grace, mercy, peace, and joy abound. I have found this to be true in both my personal walk as well as in those I coach. I also found that a breakup is exponentially less painful when there was nothing done that is supposed to be saved for a marriage union. A split after a sexual union, as many of you have experienced, has long lasting negative spiritual, emotional, mental, and sometimes even physical effects.

As many of you know, our relationship with the Lord is the wholeness of being with him. There is nothing more wonderful than being close to Jesus and giving our lives over to him completely. Jesus said, "Whoever finds their life will lose it, and whoever loses their life for my sake will find it" (Mt 10:39). We have to understand, as children of his, that it isn't just his promises of blessings and prosperity. We must understand if we want to walk with him, it is not going to be easy. Nothing worth anything ever comes easy. It may seem we have to give up a lot, but really, we are losing so little to gain so very much. God wants to know if we will lay our lives down to find a better life with him. Am I willing to completely sacrifice what I want and love for the will and love of our God? The answer is a resounding yes. Are you ready to do this? When you do this, he will give you everything. He will share his mysteries with you, he will guide you, and he will bless you beyond measure.

CONCLUSION

Now I can't promise you there won't be struggle in this process. In fact, I am absolutely promising you a battle in this journey. It's a struggle, it's painful, and at times you will have to push yourself to get motivated. As you work out your body to gain physical muscles, you work out your spirit to gain spiritual muscles. When we eat our spiritual food and vitamins, we get ripped and are able to overcome temptation and sin!

The more you can work those spiritual muscles through this book's training regime, the easier it will become. You will start gliding through your workouts, excited about how much progress you've made. Though this journey to chastity will be challenging, it can take you to the point where you are so free you will be like a carefree child again or for the first time. The good news for every step of this journey is that God is awesome, and he loves us. He goes with us into battle and will never leave us (see Dt 31:6)!

Chapter 2

RESTOCKING YOUR SPIRITUAL KITCHEN: RENEW YOUR MIND

I bet if we go into your spiritual fridge, we would be horrified at the unhealthy food in there. You've probably got some greasy burger thoughts and some fast-food french fry lies that are near impossible to digest. These are symbols for all the unhealthy, untrue thoughts that are preventing you from getting in shape spiritually.

Let me start with my old fridge of junk food. For some reason, I had always known that sex and marriage went exclusively together. This was something that was placed on my heart by God at a very early age. I didn't learn it from my family. In fact, I remember my family telling me, as Christians (and truly believing), that as long as it's "special" and you "love" the person, then sex is okay. Somehow, this just felt wrong to me at the very core of my being. However, since that sugary sweet thought was being fed to me by people I loved, there was a subconscious part of me that registered it as good for me. Unfortunately, sometimes people who love you offer things that are bad for you because they too have unhealthy eating habits. This usually passes down from generation to generation because no one learned how to eat right.

By the time I was in my twenties, all the influences, all the little "harmless" statements from family, friends, classmates, society, and media had caught up with me. I woke up one day and said, "Well, I guess I'm ready. I want to have the experience. I want to know what I'm missing. It looks like I'm not getting married anytime soon." All the lies the enemy had been working in my life for decades had finally come to fruition. I was ready to follow society and completely devalue one of the most amazing gifts God gave me: my sexuality. And guess what? I had no scriptural background, no rock foundation, and therefore no ability to fight this. I believed in Jesus. I knew God, and I knew that I loved him. However, there was a *huge* disconnect between believing in Jesus and knowing and implementing his word in my life. At that time, I had no understanding that God's word is there to protect us, to keep us safe, to show us love and help us to love ourselves and others the way that God loves us. The lies continued to pile up, and once those lies turned into actions, it was all downhill from there.

There are seven major lies of the enemy that keep us from purity and chastity. All of them come up often with those I coach. I'm going to list each one so you can determine which junk food you are eating and toss it into the garbage disposal. After each lie, I will share with you the Truth of Christ so you are able to reframe your mind and restock your spiritual kitchen. Once you have a healthy mind diet,

you will be much more prepared to succeed in this journey
to chastity!

LIE 1

*"I'm not perfect. I'm only human and I'm weak, so I can't do
that. I could never be chaste like you. I'm not good enough."*

Now, as Mr. Wonderful would say on Shark Tank, throw
out that "nothing burger!" Take that nothing burger out
of your mouth and out of your heart and mind right now!
Because that is what that lie will get you. Nothing! Do you
hear the immediate limitation we put on ourselves and
on God when we believe this lie? In some churches, we so
often hear about not putting limits on what God can give us
in terms of money, jobs, success, and other worldly goods.

Well, I suggest a greater and more powerful limitless-
ness! There is no limit to the level of holiness and goodness God can give to you and your life and ways. Yes, we
as humans are limited in our flesh, but when we operate by
the spirit, there are no limits to what can be done in us.

My personal journey is a perfect example. There was no
way I ever thought I could get back that childlike innocence. "And he said: 'Truly I tell you, unless you change
and become like little children, you will never enter the
kingdom of heaven'" (Mt 18:3). I remember being very
young and never thinking anything lustful on a date. It
never even crossed my mind. Are you able to think back
to a time many years ago when your thoughts were so pure
that even if you were in a situation of temptation, you never

even considered having sex with someone? (If that is where you are currently, great! Stay there!) God has returned me to that purity through the gifts of the Holy Spirit, and he will bring you back too. "The fruit of the Spirit is love, joy, peace, forbearance, kindness, goodness, faithfulness, gentleness and self-control" (Gal 5:22–23). The greater the Holy Spirit is within you and sanctifying grace, the greater the supernatural ability to overcome sin, especially the sins of lust and sexual sin. I am a living testament to this being true.

LIE 2

"I can't be pure because I've done too many bad things. It's too late for me."

This is the other one that I've heard a lot in coaching, and even one I told myself. It's always the same response at first. "Oh, I can't be pure and chaste. I've done too many bad things. I'm not as good and holy as you." The enemy, society, other people, and our own minds have ingrained the lie that change is not possible.

Sometimes people don't show up until the end of the movie where they only see the happy ending. They never see the blood, sweat, tears, and struggle that got them to that happy, successful place. We all have to start at the bottom and climb our way up to the top of the mountain. It's an amazing workout, and I know from the top of the purity mountain that if I can make it up here, so can you and so can anyone. I'm not better or holier than anyone else. Most importantly, I've been where you are right now. It looks daunting, but when you win in Christ, that victory is so sweet!

From the atheist to the most conservative and devout Christian, this lie permeates many minds. Early on in my journey to chastity, I had an atheist tell me that since I wasn't a virgin anymore, it was too late for me and there was no reason to be chaste. I also had a conservative Christian condemn me, telling me that I should feel awful about what I had done in the past. If I still felt awful about it and hadn't accepted God's forgiveness, I would have condemned myself and would never have been able to pull myself out of that hole that the enemy had prepared for me. If I believed it was too late, it would have stopped me in my tracks right then and there. That's exactly what Satan wants you to think, that you have fallen too far to ever make a comeback. It's the perfect strategy of an enemy in wartime, and he will use anyone he can to convey that message. Ignore those lies and remember God's word is always true. He promises time and time again that anytime we are willing to turn back and repent, he will forgive us and restore us and make us anew.

The truth is God has removed our sins as far from us as the east is from the west (see Ps 103:12). In Deuteronomy 30, God says, if "you and your children return to the Lord your God and obey him with all your heart and with all your soul according to everything I command you today, then the LORD your God will restore your fortunes and have compassion on you and gather you again from all the nations where he scattered you" (vv. 2–3).

In Hebrews 8:12, we are even told that God will "forgive their wickedness and will remember their sins no more." As humans, we have the old adage of "forgive but don't forget." God doesn't work that way. He literally will wipe the slate clean. It brings happy tears to my eyes to know that this is the truth of the Lord! I cherish it and live in that truth every day, and I pray through this journey that you will come to do the same.

Jeremiah 29:11 has that famous passage about God having a plan for us, not to harm us, but to give us hope and a future. But what he says right after that is even more amazing! He says, "'Then you will call on me and come and pray to me, and I will listen to you. You will seek me and find me when you seek me with all your heart. I will be found by you,' declares the LORD, 'and will bring you back from captivity. I will gather you from all the nations and places where I have banished you,' declares the LORD, 'and will bring you back to the place from which I carried you into exile'" (Jer 29:12–14).

So as long as we have breath in our bodies, it is never too late to turn back, to change our ways. Now, when people say to me, "Oh, you're so good and pure," it's because they didn't know me before my profound conversion. They also didn't see the long period of time I spent in the darkness being prepared and struggling to become the chaste person God made me today.

When I share my testimony with those I coach, I always get a shocked reaction. "No, you never could have been like that. It's hard to believe." Many who knew me before and after have since changed their lives, including some non-believers. They saw the Holy Spirit transform me to such a profound extent before their eyes that they thought it humanly impossible for someone to change that much. Therefore, by means of intellectual deduction, there must have been something bigger at work than human will.

Testimony

A man I was coaching was living with his girlfriend. When he started soaking up the Bible like a sponge and decided to get baptized, I was ecstatic because I knew all the great things that were ahead for him. Shortly after his baptism, the Holy Spirit convicted his heart that the relationship he was in was not being handled in a godly way. The man, who wasn't even thinking of getting married for many years to come, now was asking his girlfriend to marry him and live out his relationship in a godly way.

We all make mistakes and sin. One of the most wonderful things about the Lord is that he lets us right the wrong. And if we are truly sorry and change our ways, he washes us clean and makes us white as snow. Now my friend just had his one year anniversary with his wife. They are so happy together, and he said the relationship is so much better and more blessed now that he's doing things God's way instead of the world's way or his way.

LIE 3

"But my body needs the release, and it isn't right to deny my body what it wants. It's natural."

Capital N to the O. That's like saying pizza is healthy because it has all the food groups. It sounds great and we want to believe it because it's so yummy, but it's simply not true. Pizza is going to show negatively on your body pretty quickly, just like sexual sin shows negatively in your spirit.

I used to say this lie myself when I couldn't stop sinning years ago. I was doing my best to justify it because even though I wanted to stop, I couldn't. I had never been addicted to anything in my entire life, so when I was not able to just quit cold turkey, I felt ashamed. I used this lie to try to justify why I couldn't stop. At that time, I was still lacking some wisdom regarding the absolute value of my purity to God and how Satan was going to do anything and everything he could to destroy it. Even my attempts to live God's way were miserable because I would fail and then spiral down into feeling guilty and hating myself for it. Living in God's freedom now, I know for a fact that my body doesn't need it. I'm totally healthy, happy, and out of bondage. To this day, from the moment God freed me years ago (and it was a moment I will explain in a later chapter), I have never even thought about doing that. It never even crosses my mind, except in great thanks for that freedom.

I will never forget, though, how awful that struggle was and using that justification. It's one of the reasons why it was important to write this book, so that lie gets busted and incinerated in as many lives and minds as God reaches with these pages.

LIE 4

"Wouldn't God want me to make my partner happy?"

Jesus wants us to love each other. He said, "A new command I give you: Love one another. As I have loved you, so you must love one another" (Jn 13:34).

If we truly love others, we don't want to defile them in any way. If we love someone, we wouldn't want to hurt or lead a partner into temptation, but rather have that person delivered from evil. The purity of our hearts and minds is how we embody Jesus's love and how we make a home for him in our hearts so we may live out Gods will.

Jesus also never wants you to do anything for your partner that goes against his words and his teachings. He also wouldn't want you to have a partner who would encourage you to sin and go against God's word.

Acting on this lie is idolatry, because you are putting what a person wants above what God wants. It's something I personally used to be very guilty of in relationships. God and the body of Christ had to reveal to me that when we put anything above or in front of God's love, his words, and his teachings, we are creating idols. "You shall have no other gods before me" (Ex 20:3). It's the very first commandment of the Ten Commandments. It is wrong to love anyone so much as to be unwilling to lose them for the sake of Christ and his love (see Mk 10:29; Mt 16:24–25; Lk 17:33).

In coaching, I often hear, "Well I've never found anyone that doesn't try to get me to do sexual things with them. I just haven't found anyone who wants to be pure with me." I have found, however, that the stronger you get in your own purity, the more you will attract partners who are like-minded, or willing to be.

If "passion takes over and all else is out the window," then something may be missing in your prayer life. The flesh should never be stronger than the spirit of a Christian, and we will work together to make sure this is true for you. "You, dear children, are from God and have overcome them, because the one who is in you is greater than the one who is in the world" (1 Jn 4:4).

In a union that is truly ordained by God, your chastity and commitment to God, not sexual immorality, should make your partner happy. If you have a partner who is trying to tempt you into breaking your chastity, then that partner needs to work on their own spiritual life before being in a relationship led by God. If he or she is not willing to work on that, then that person may not be God's best for your future spouse . . . at least at the present time.

LIE 5

"The Bible is from thousands of years ago. That was then and this is now."

We hear this all the time in society. "Well, things were different back then. We were living in a different time, and society has changed, and we have to get with the modern age. Now it's okay to have sex outside of marriage and not be so old fashioned."

In reality, the Bible is as relevant today as it was two thousand years ago, as it will be two thousand years from now. Times can change to where we will be driving flying cars, and God's word will still remain the same. With the Lord, today is like a thousand years, and a thousand years a day (see 2 Pt 3:8). Anything outside of God's word, we will eventually suffer for in the long run, in this world or the next.

Scripture is very clear about sexual immorality in the Old Testament, and Jesus confirms this in the four Gospels. He is the way, truth, and life (see Jn 14:6). He is the only way. There are wonderful biblical passages to meditate on in the chapter 6 devotional to really fill your heart and mind with the truth. I can personally testify from my own journey that once I started following the biblical rules regarding sexuality, my life and my relationships completely transformed. I am now at the point that I would never even want to turn back. I've been on both sides, and there is absolutely no comparison. The truth of the faith is the way to go, and the peace, joy, and blessings that will result are limitless.

Your relationship with Jesus will be better and stronger. When you close a door to major sin in your life, you give God the opportunity to bless you more and give you more. Having sex outside of marriage (or engaging in other sexual sins between A and Z) is like praying with clenched fists. Try this right now. Put your hands out in front of you, like you are going to receive a gift, and clench both hands into fists. If someone tried to hand you something now and give you a present, are you able to grab it? Now open your hands. When your hands are open, you can easily and flawlessly receive gifts the Lord wants to hand you. So stretch out your hands and receive the gifts God wants to give you.

LIE 6

"You are missing out on the most amazing thing ever."

Satan always lies with half-truths to make us stumble. Remember the enemy has "no truth in him. When he lies, he speaks his native language, for he is a liar and the father of lies" (Jn 8:44).

Yes, sex is the most amazing thing ever in the context that God created it for: marriage. Satan always twists what is beautiful and pure. It is only the most amazing gift if you don't curse it and your relationship. When we go against God's plan and God's will for our lives and his teachings, we suffer deeply for it.

Nothing outside of God's will is going to turn out well. Unless we do things his way, we are in agreement with the enemy. Unfortunately, the enemy's full-time job is to steal, kill, and destroy. Satan tempts us so that we agree to something that gives him legal authority to destroy us. In fact, he's so crafty that we actually destroy ourselves. We do have our free will, so we can choose God's way or we can choose our own way.

When it comes to sex, if we do things our way, we only

receive temporary enjoyment from it and that enjoyment is then gone. We can keep going back again to try and relive that temporary pleasure, only to find that, ultimately, it is an empty pleasure, and finally, no pleasure at all. The reason it is empty is because we are taking the most beautiful thing that God gave us, and we are defiling and deforming it according to what we want. We are replacing God's perfect design with our own imperfect one. And that's what the enemy does. He can't create. He can only offer counterfeits, so he twists the beautiful thing or image that God has created. He makes it look shiny on the outside, but once we pull the curtain back, we end up very sad, very lost, and very broken. What we thought was beautiful is now twisted as you are operating in the enemy camp, where everything is turned to dust and light is turned to darkness.

I can testify to this because I've been there. I've been exactly where you may be right now. God turned it around for me once I committed to him. He will do that for you also. He's been using my mistakes and my pain for good to help others. That's what is so wonderful about the Lord. He's waiting for us to come back to him so he can "make all things work together for our good." Now, I'm not saying it won't be a struggle getting back to him. All that darkness takes time to shed, but the good news is there is light at the end of the tunnel, and I can testify that once you come out on the other side, it is the most beautiful, joyful, and exciting place to be.

LIE 7

"There is a lot of fun still to be had between A and Z."

When you are first becoming chaste, or if you are still a virgin, there is a lot to navigate. It reminds me of when we were kids and sexual activity was compared to baseball bases. Remember? "Did you get to third base?" The truth is, I don't think God really likes baseball in this regard. Everyone clearly has their own definition of chastity, but I'm pretty sure God's definition is not Bill Clinton's definition.

This is a truth that takes time though. In recently coaching someone, he told me he can stop having sex, but he doesn't think he can go without C and D on the menu. These grey areas are something that the Holy Spirit has to convict each of our hearts on, and it takes time. For me, with each relationship after my chastity, God kept pushing me back further and further to take me further and further toward him. As your heart changes, you will feel more convicted about each base. Like Bill Murray in *What About Bob?* sometimes it's baby steps to the door, baby steps to full purity.

CONTINUE IN TRUTH

While the above are seven principal lies that must be rooted out from our minds to arrive at chastity in mind and body, there will later be many additional, albeit not so obvious, lies that must be replaced with Christ's truth.

Fighting for physical chastity can be such a huge war,

I found it was crucial to focus on that for the salvation of my very soul. However, after my physical chastity was in place, there were new ways that I was then able to grow in healthiness and holiness. I share a few of these with you to encourage you in the future that God has prepared for you.

Coming home from war is a process and there is unfortunate spiritual and emotional aftermath. For me, here are some of the main lies I have been able to replace with truth, since my physical freedom. Some of these may ring true for you, but if you are like me, they were so buried, I had to dig through the layers with the Holy Spirit to overcome the effects and even the original reasons for my sexual sin.

> In Jesus's Name,
> I renounce the lie that I'm worthless;
> I renounce the lie that I'm only worth my sexuality;
> I renounce the lie that no one would love me or want me for me;
> I renounce the lie that I'm ruined for a relationship because of my past sexual sin;
> I renounce the lie that it's hopeless;
> I renounce the lie that I'm not good enough;
> I renounce the lie that I don't deserve love, a good husband, or family;
> I renounce the lie that men will only be interested in me if I dress immodestly. (Truth: I don't want that type of man.)

Ultimately, it's imperative that as you read this book and live the forty-day devotional, you envision yourself as the beautiful person God made you and that God intended you to be. It's always hard to see the light sometimes during the process. I will be here to remind you of that light and encourage you as your personal trainer through this book, to walk with you into new levels of purity with Christ leading the way. Your spiritual muscles are going to be so strong that there will be no stopping you and you will fly to heights you may not be able to fully realize right now.

Now that we have our mind right, it's time to get into some serious spiritual workouts. So take a breather, get some holy water, and get ready to turn your spiritual physique into that of an Olympic contender!

Chapter 3

STRENGTH TRAINING: FORGIVENESS

FOR those of us on this adventure toward chastity and overall holiness, forgiveness is like the Holy Grail to Indiana Jones or "my precious" to Smeagol in *Lord of the Rings*. It unleashes a palpable spiritual power. In training those spiritual muscles, lack of forgiveness is to your spirit what blocked arteries are to your heart. You are going to have major trouble making strides and progress due to symptoms including shortness of breath (of life) and early fatigue.

Our goal here is to unblock your heart so everything can flow from it and you can succeed in this journey to purity faster and easier than ever before. We are going to do this in an easy four-step process. If you commit to it, this is an absolutely life changing process. When you are finished, you will feel spiritually lighter, as if you had lost twenty pounds, and you will be free to move in the spirit towards the heart of purity you desire.

CONFESS

It's very important to confess our sins to God. It's also very important to confess our sin to someone else. James says, "Therefore confess your sins to each other and pray for each other so that you may be healed. The prayer of a righteous person is powerful and effective" (Jas 5:16).

So often I see this as a stumbling block for overcoming sexual sin, especially with "self-gratification" or pornography. There is a major inability to heal due to the private nature of these two sexual sins. A person can be stuck in that bondage for many years because it is done in the darkness. When you confess it to another, it brings the sin out into the open, and once it is in the light, the real healing is able to occur. The Lord says that "whatever is hidden is meant to be disclosed, and whatever is concealed is meant to be brought out into the open" (Mk 4:22).

There is another amazing part of this process: many people feel fine confessing alone directly to God but are actually far more humbled in having to confess a sin to another human being, especially when that person is someone they spiritually respect or even admire.

Testimonial: Spiritual Bondage

I was helping a man in his mid-twenties who was a virgin but struggling with his flesh desire to have sex and give up his true God desire to wait for marriage. With no wife in sight, he was really on the verge of falling. However, his main issue was one that he had kept a secret for three years. He had been having a serious spiritual struggle with masturbation. He felt guilty and he felt unclean. The reason why this sin can be even harder to break than sexually sinning with a partner is because it is a very private sin. It not only can be kept hidden for a long time but can be a greater struggle because it seems to be a very taboo subject that is rarely discussed openly. Once he shared this with me, he brought that darkness into the light. Satan cannot live in the light and loses his power. In this way, he was no longer alone in the battle for his soul. I was able to encourage him and pray in agreement for this bondage to be broken in Jesus's name. "Again, truly I tell you that if two of you on earth agree about anything they ask for, it will be done for them by my Father in heaven" (Mt 18:19). Within a few weeks, I received a call from him saying that it was the first time he had made progress in that area in the three years of hidden bondage.

ASK

Make sure you ask God to forgive *all* your past sexual sins. I guarantee, unless you were really super human in your walk up to this point, you have forgotten something. I'm not going to get into all of them. The Holy Spirit will convict your heart of what you need to confess in this area. I am going to teach you to do an exercise to make sure you have them all covered. Grab a notebook and a pen. Go to your prayer altar, prayer room, or wherever you go to hear

God the clearest and have the most quiet so you are able to listen for that still small voice to guide you. Now take your time with this. It could take you an hour, a few days, or even a week, depending on your age. Spend time in prayer, as I emphasized in the last chapter, and write down the names of every single person you had any unhealthy sexual relationship with. This includes lustful thoughts and all lustful actions outside of marriage. You may not even remember all of them, so ask the Holy Spirit to reveal anyone you may have forgotten. Ask forgiveness for all of these. If there is anyone or anything you may not remember, be sure to include at the end: "and anyone and anything I don't remember." The point of this exercise is to be pure of heart and come to God openly and honestly and lay it all at the foot of the cross for him to forgive you and take it from you. This is the time to really clear out this part of your life and start completely fresh and new with God. Let the Holy Spirit fill those areas now forgiven with the light and love of Jesus Christ.

GIVE

For our next step in this healing process to chastity, we must forgive *every* person who has hurt us in our past. The Lord says in the New Testament, not only is it not "eye for an eye" anymore, we are also not even allowed to be angry with our brother or sister (see Mt 5:22). As God forgives us, we must also forgive all others (see Mk 11:25; Col 3:13).

I was at a fellowship lunch with a girl who had recently

broken up with her boyfriend. About three months had passed since he had ended it in a very unhealthy and less than kind manner. As we were talking, she mentioned that new information about her ex-boyfriend had recently come to light. She told me how she can't believe he did this particular thing and that it may have been going on during their relationship. As she was sharing the story, she was rubbing her neck and telling me how she's had horrible neck pain the past few days. I asked her if it started around the same time that she found out about this new information. She said, "Yes, shortly after. Why?" It's amazing how much we can physically hold in our bodies from not forgiving people, both physically and spiritually. Sometimes we don't even realize we haven't forgiven the person. Then, a light bulb went off as her eyes widened with the realization. She yelped, "Oh my goodness, have I not forgiven him?" Fast forward a few days later to where she, through prayer, forgave him. When she released that pain and negativity in her spirit, she also released it in her body and her neck went back to normal.

I am the perfect example of someone who struggled to forgive others. It was a major issue in my life, and my journey to chastity began the very first day I was able to start forgiving others. This was the first major conversion of my heart. I had two, but this was the first. I was sitting in church. I had been attending services every Sunday for about six months at this point. On this particular day, I had gone to service only to discover that the regular pastor was not there. Instead, the service was to be led by the business pastor. I thought to myself, "Oh great. What a wasted morning. What could a business pastor possibly say to help me on my journey? I'm trying to change here." I actually almost left early. Thankfully, the Holy Spirit didn't let me leave, and to this day, it is one of the two best messages I have ever heard in a sermon or homily. He started to speak about Jesus's walk to Calvary and explained how even though in all the visuals Jesus is wearing a loin cloth, in actuality, he was naked for that walk.[1] I had heard stories of Jesus, but this was something I had never heard before. He continued to explain that they stripped him naked to shame him, embarrass him, and make him feel worthless.

The pastor then related this to all the things that people have done to us to make us feel that way and that no matter what, we couldn't let it work. We couldn't be shamed and we couldn't be made worthless. For the first time in five years, I started to cry. I cried five years' worth of tears in this one sitting and was uncontrollably sobbing. All the Christians around me were so nice they were patting me on the shoulder and trying to give me tissues. It got so bad though, I finally had to run out because I just couldn't stop crying, but when I did, I felt free. I felt free for maybe the first time in many years since I hit puberty.

All the men that tried to make me worth nothing more

---

[1]   I am not certain that the pastor was right about Jesus being naked during the way of the Cross, but I am grateful for him and his sermon that day as it truly changed my life.

than the way I looked. All the guys that had treated me like I wasn't worth more than my body and all the years they did this before I even believed them or gave into that in my mid-twenties. From when I was thirteen to twenty-five years old, guy after guy told me I wasn't worth knowing, with or without words, and rather only worth what I looked like and how I could be a trophy or toy for them. They could play with me and then put me on a shelf, as long as I didn't have any real thoughts or feelings to bother them with.

Over and over again this message was repeated to me until, in my twenties, I figured if I can't beat them, join them. I thought I might as well just be exactly who they want me to be. It was a mistake that could have been fatal to my eternal life and maybe my life here on earth. It was a mistaken identity, which would have continued had I not heard that sermon. It was in that moment, for the first time in as long as I could remember, that I knew my worth in Jesus Christ. I was loved and valued and anything that a man thought simply didn't matter anymore. More importantly, I related to what Jesus had gone through and I knew how he felt in his humanity, what he was willing to go through for us and our salvation. In this moment, which was the first big step on my journey to giving my life to Christ, I could forgive all those men who had done that to me. I wasn't angry anymore. A huge weight just lifted off me. I was free in Christ Jesus.

That was a major change in my heart that made me

realize I still had other people in other areas in my life I needed to forgive. Here's the life changing method I used.

Exercise to Forgive

A wonderful priest taught me this many years ago when I first converted. I was trying to change my life to live for the Lord and struggling terribly with forgiveness. I use it to this day to help me, and now I am able, with Christ, to forgive everyone.

Please use this exercise. It works.

Step 1: Go to a quiet place with just you and the Lord, or you can do this with a friend to help you along.

Step 2: Start with the most recent person that hurt you and work backwards to your earliest memory. (If you need to do this in separate sessions, that is fine also. Rome wasn't built in a day.)

Step 3: Now close your eyes and picture you are in a room with Jesus. Visualize the most recent person you need to forgive walking into that room. Now go give them a hug, say you forgive them, and then give them to Jesus.

This may take time and that's okay. Some will take five seconds, and others could take a lot longer. Some you may have to come back to multiple times. You may even originally visualize yourself crying or yelling (or worse) instead of hugging that person you are trying to forgive. It doesn't matter the time it takes. This process is about being able to give them the forgiveness *you* need and letting Jesus take over from here with them.

Important note: Remember, as you pray and reflect, there are byproducts of lack of forgiveness. Make sure you also renounce and release any anger, hatred, resentment, bitterness, and judgement that tend to hang out with an unforgiving spirit.

Again, take your time and have mercy with yourself in the process. I've learned along the way that major betrayals are forgiven in layers. Some good questions to ask yourself along the way to see how deep that forgiveness is going are: Do you wish that person bad or want to harm them? Have you stopped thinking about that person/trauma or are you still stewing over what happened? Are you able to offer up your suffering for their salvation? Are you able to beg God to forgive them?

Jesus said, "Father, forgive them, for they know not what they are doing" (Lk 23:34). This seems to be the deepest level of forgiveness and the heart of Jesus Christ. This will come for you over time, as it did for me. Keep leaving it at the foot of the cross until you don't pick it up again, truly giving it over to Jesus.

Step 4: Now repeat this with every person you need to forgive, moving backwards through your life.

Step 5: Walk into freedom with a changed heart and continue to allow the Holy Spirit to now fill those recesses with more of Jesus's love. I believe it was Mother Teresa that used to ask Jesus to lend her his heart. What a beautiful and powerful prayer request.

RELEASE YOURSELF

This is the primary setback I see in a lot of Christians' progress. Holding onto sin is like carrying around a backpack full of dumbbell weights. The more sins, the more weights are in the backpack. The more dumbbells you have, the more it drags you down and the less you can accomplish in your faith journey. Let's say I'm your best friend. I see you suffering and struggling with the weight of these loaded backpacks, so of course, caring about you, I'm going to come over and ask if I can take the backpack from you and release you from that heavy load.

That's what Jesus does. He died for our sins so that we could be free. When Jesus died on the cross for us, it was for our sins and to take the weight (burden) of those sins from us.

There are a lot of you out there who have forgiven others and even know that God has forgiven you, but you are unable to forgive yourself. The Holy Spirit used me to minister to a young woman in her mid-twenties who has a special testimony and gift in speaking to youth. She got into a bad crowd in her teen years and ended up drinking, drugging, and getting into crime and the industry of strip clubs and prostitution. Ten years later, she has completely turned her life around and is now a healthy gym girl who never drinks or smokes, is married, and holds a legitimate job. Yet she says she somehow can't get close to God like others have. She tells me with the absolute sweetest demeanor that somehow, she just doesn't make the progress that other Christians make in their walk.

Here's the problem. She's still living in the past. She cannot forgive herself for the awful things she did and what she put her family through so many years ago. Not forgiving herself is keeping her in bondage and she can't break free. When I tell her she has to forgive herself, she tells me she did too many bad things, so she feels guilty all the time. She feels that she is the reason that her father died, from the stress of knowing his daughter was such a mess. So I tell her that she cannot carry that weight and that she must give it to God. She says, "That's what my brother keeps telling me."

At that moment, the Holy Spirit moves in and speaks through me with such force as I see a gym towel on her shoulder. So I say to her, "Give me your towel." She starts to hand it to me, but then as we are both holding the towel, she says, "No, you can't have it." And I said, "Why? Give me the towel," and we are both trying to hold the towel. Then she just calls out to me like a small child and says, "But it's dirty! I can't give it to you because it's dirty." We just looked at each other and I said, "That's exactly what you're doing to God. He wants to take that dirty towel from you, which is your past, but you are too scared to give it to him. You think it's too dirty for God to hold and carry."

Just then both our eyes welled up with tears and her entire body was covered in Holy Spirit chills. You could see something clicked with her and changed before my eyes.

Something she had not been able to reconcile in ten years. Now, for the first time, she has a chance to let go of her past life. I tell this wonderful hearted woman, "You are free, because you asked for forgiveness. God forgives you so you are white as snow." I look in her eyes and know she could now see the light at the end of a very dark tunnel.

If your story is like this, then the main thing for you personally to work on is to root yourself more in the Word of God. Who does God tell you that you are? Once you know your identity in Christ and how special you are to him, how much he loves you unconditionally, and how forgiven you are, then you can release that weight. Then you can move into the promises of Christ Jesus. "Therefore, if anyone is in Christ, the new creation has come: The old has gone, the new is here!" (2 Cor 5:17). Let's hear an Amen!

Now having done these four steps, you are able to walk in the freedom of forgiveness. That freedom provides the ability for God to now work fully in your heart and bring you to that blissful place of purity.

Chapter 4

STAMINA BUILDING AND SPIRITUAL SCULPTING: POWER OF PRAYER AND FASTING

NOW it's time to gear up for some definition of our spiritual muscles! Some of you may look ripped on the outside, but what's more important is how you look on the inside. Have you ever seen the Jack Black movie *Shallow Hal*? It's about a man who only used to care about looks but is now only able to see what people look like on the inside. So a woman with the physical beauty of a ten would look like a three to Hal if her heart, soul, and spirit were not where they needed to be. If Hal were to look at you right now, what would your spirit look like to him? Would you be flexing those biceps or quads or are you looking more like a couch potato? Are you winning the 10k run or are you huffing and puffing walking to the next room?

Our prayer lives are to our spiritual strength what a can of spinach is to Popeye's physical strength. When I'm praying in the morning, I often say I've got to get my Popeye's spinach and then watch all my spiritual muscles pop up so I'm ready to face the day. We can also compare our prayer lives to a soldier in wartime. Would you go into the middle of a war zone without your protective helmet, your bullet-proof vest, and all of your boot camp and daily training?

Now, no matter where you are starting today, it is enough for Jesus! He is just glad you are here and ready to begin your spiritual regimen or take it to the next level. It doesn't matter if you are spiritually starting this journey as a pro ball player or the class klutz. Having a willing heart that says, "Put me in coach!" is all that he asks. God always meets us right where we are! Whether you start with cross fit mania or take it slow with Richard Simmons "Dancing to the Oldies," God has you covered.

Now it's time to get down to serious business. Our prayer lives are directly correlated to our ability to rule over sin. Stamina, by definition, is the ability to sustain prolonged physical or mental effort. The more you build up your stamina, the higher level of spiritual fitness you will be able to achieve. Since we can't be expected to immediately jump from running ten minutes a day on the treadmill to an hour a day without wiping out, we need to do the same in our spiritual workouts to build up to your peak performance. So, whereas we may run on a treadmill for twenty minutes a day and then increase to thirty minutes and so on, we will apply the same principal to ramp up our spiritual cardio ability. By the end of this boot camp, you won't be anything less than the spiritual warrior God knows you are.

Now there are two parts to this workout: *prayer and fasting*, which we'll cover in separate sections. Prayer must be daily, but the more you can intertwine fasting into your life, the better. There is nothing cooler or better in your stamina workout than going double Dutch. Seriously, how much cooler were the kids dancing and jumping over the extra obstacle with ease and joy than the kid on the sideline with the single jump rope. I'd rather get to the point where we have fun making the difficult complexity look like child's play!

The devotional in chapter 6, "Forty Days to a Heart of Purity," is to keep your heart and mind focused. It will help you get through the wilderness stage, just like the forty days that Jesus wandered in the desert before coming to his full potential. You can start the devotional after this chapter, or you can read all the chapters first to understand the full plan and then dive in to chapter 6. In this section, you'll receive some keys to unlock the kingdom's full power to make you a powerhouse in forty days. Remembering and incorporating these points during the devotional will help make it the most effective as you turn your struggle into ease.

PRAYER TIME AND FOCUS

The higher the quality of your prayer, both in time and in focus, the more God is able to act in your life and in your temple. Whenever possible, we need our main prayer time to be during the day when we are our strongest, not our weakest, with concentrated prayer and fervor. Everyone has a different time for peak performance. Mine is first thing in the morning before I get distracted with other things—phone, emails, family, etc. I even know some prayer warriors (and I do this on occasion) who wake up at 4 a.m., like the biblical prophets, and pray then. There's certainly nothing to distract them at that time. However, some of you are night people, and sitting down for your prayer time late at night is when you have the most energy and focus.

If you are not able, due to your life circumstance, to pray at your peak time, just do the best you can. You may have a mini-me (or three or eight!) running around or be in the midst of a huge school/work project at your peak energy time. The point is trying your best, when at all possible, to avoid making prayer your last priority. We have to remember God wants our first fruits. He desires to be the center and most important thing in our lives. Whenever I start to put my time with God at the end of the list, he always leads me back to Genesis 4 when he explains through Cain and Abel when he does not look upon Cain's offering with favor that "if you do what is right, will you not be accepted? But if you do not do what is right, sin is crouching at your door." He desires our first fruits always. In Genesis 4, Abel brings God a choice offering, and God was pleased. However, God wasn't happy with Cain's offering and knew Cain could give more to him.

God understands we all have busy lives, but he also doesn't want us so busy that we don't have time for him. Everything we have and do is from him and because of him. When Mary sat at Jesus's feet while Martha worried herself and ran around like a busy bee because there was so much to do, Jesus said Mary made the better choice (see Lk 10:38–42). Aside from being too busy with daily to-dos, we also need to be careful about not putting prayer after leisure time. For example, we don't want to watch hours of television then pray only for a few minutes and fall asleep before we even finish. If that's what is being done, we cannot reach our goals. God gives us as much as we are willing to put into our faith journey. The more we focus on him, the more ready we are to receive all the great wonders and blessings he has to bestow on us.

I recently started working with a girl who was struggling in a particular sexual sin. In getting to the bottom of it, I asked how long she was praying each day. She said, "Twenty minutes every morning." A person exercising for twenty minutes a day is going to be in decent shape. It's a lot more than many people are doing, but it's not what the champion athletes are doing. If you want to be a spiritual athlete, you need to train like an athlete. I'm here to make you an athlete so that in the power of the Holy Spirit, God will be able to run circles around the enemy, his temptations, and his tactics coming against you.

Now you should not, in any way, take a legalistic approach to prayer. If you want to get your prayers up to an hour a day, it's not something you want to time out exactly or it would become a religious rule. One day you may get in only forty-five minutes of solid quiet time with Jesus, but another day you feel so on fire you keep praying and Bible study for an hour and a half. Overall, we want to spend as much time with the Father as possible.

PRAY WITHOUT CEASING

The Bible says to pray without ceasing (see 1 Thes 5:17). Now, obviously, if we were praying only in concentrated prayer all day, we wouldn't get any of our this-world activities done. God, of course, deserves every second as everything flows from him. Every worldly possession we have is only because God provided it. The key here then is to do both. Keep focused on God in everything you do during the day and every free moment just check in with the Lord, thanking him, praising him, and asking him for guidance in every decision.

Make sure he has the wheel and is leading the way. I learned about four years ago to repeat in my mind: "I love you Lord. I praise you Lord. I trust you Lord." I also always call on the Holy Spirit to represent God well to others and for his light to shine through us and on us. Of course, your relationship is personal, and you will have your own personal dialogue with him.

YOUR WILL BE DONE

We have to ask the Lord to do his will, not ours. As Jesus said during his agony in the garden, "Yet not my will, but yours be done" (Lk 22:42). This is a huge issue that comes up when I'm coaching and find people "stuck" at a certain

point and not seeing the results they should be seeing. I was
trying to help a man at one time who was as high up in the
military as possible. He was a Catholic and wanted to do
things God's way, but he was so used to exerting his own
physical and mental force over military situations, it was
very difficult for him to give God the wheel to change his
life and heart. Often times, though, we have to let go and let
God. Yes, I know that is easier said than done. It is a crucial
part of the process though.

Interestingly, in all I've seen, it also tends to be easier
for women to give up control than men. You gentlemen,
as you are created, like to take the lead and want to be in
control. This was something that I struggled with at the
beginning of my journey because I was very much "guy
like" in my past life. I always wanted to control, fix, and
exert my will to correct any situation or problem. The issue
with that is this is a God territory and God solution. For
you to both overcome your flesh and overcome the enemy's temptations and harassment, it cannot be through
your own human power. It indeed has to fully be in the
name of Jesus Christ, through the power of the Holy Spirit,
and the infinite mercy and grace from God almighty. "With
man this is impossible, but with God all things are possible"
(Mt 19:26). If you feel that no matter what you do you can't
seem to break whatever type of sexual sin is the weakness,
it is likely because you are still fighting in the flesh and hav-
en't given it over to God to fight the battle for you. Only
God can do this for you. We will take all the steps we can

and then let him work his miracle as he did for me and many others. Your miracle is coming!

Willpower Testimonial: Free From Pornography

(Personal account post spiritual coaching)

"Since I was a teenager, I struggled with an addiction to pornography. Long before I ever had my first girlfriend, pornography was my first girlfriend. Even before I was a Christian, I knew deep down that there was something morally wrong with pornography, and I could see the ways it would negatively influence some of my thoughts and actions. But I didn't have a full understanding of why this was.

"Once I accepted Jesus into my heart and started reading and following his word, I learned that pornography was adultery in the heart (see Mt 5:27–28) and contrary to his design for me. I knew that my behavior was something that was going to have to change. However, even as I worked to clean up other parts of my life and make them right with the Lord, my addiction to pornography was the one thing that I couldn't shake. No matter how hard an effort I put up to stop, I couldn't on my own power. I would last as long as my willpower would hold up. But then something would always happen that would make me slip up.

"Through Nicole's help and coaching, I learned the flaw in my approach. I was trying to make my actions right with God, but I was trying to do so only through my own ability, without seeking God's help and guidance through the process. So even though my heart and intentions were in the right place, I would ultimately fail because I was trying to fight a spiritual battle with human means. It was only once Nicole showed me how to fight my problem through spiritual means like prayer and fasting instead of just trying to rely on my own willpower, that I started to see real gains. My freedom from pornography didn't happen overnight. It took time and dedication, but by staying dedicated to prayer and focusing on God, I was eventually able to gain control over my addiction and defeat it."

WE HAVE TO PRAY RIGHT

If we pray for something that we *want*, then we are not trusting God. We are thinking we know what's best for ourselves. The truth is only God knows what is best for us and sees the full picture of our lives. We should instead be praying his will for our lives and that he uses us as his instruments. Primarily, praying right is highlighted in the Lord's Prayer (see Mt 6:9-13). Holy is Your Name. Give us our daily bread, forgive us our sins, help us to forgive others, deliver us from evil, and lead us not into temptation. This should be how we are praying, as Jesus taught us.

I was so in love with my high school sweetheart that I literally prayed for us to be back together. I'm so relentless that I literally bugged God for ten years to give him back to me. God finally got so frustrated with me, he gave me exactly what I wanted! That engagement was literally in the top three worst things that ever happened to me. It was an absolute disaster match, and boy, did I learn my lesson. When you hear the saying, be careful what you wish for, be careful what you *pray* for. God had to respect my free will and allowed me to have what I went after. This revealed to me that, all those years, he was trying to protect me by *not* giving me what I wanted most. I learned one of the greatest lessons ever, and that is if God doesn't give us something that we want, it's because he has a better plan for us and he knows who we need, which is far more important than who we want.

PRAISE HIM IN THE SUN AND IN THE STORM

I find little more powerful than praising the Lord in the storm. Finding peace on that boat with Jesus, with the wind and rain beating down on you, is the most powerful praise and thanksgiving there is. Anyone can praise God in the good times. It's easy to thank God when everything is going great and perfect. When you can do the same absolute thanking in the midst of a Job experience, well then, that is true devotion and praise. This type of prayer is what changes your life. A huge paradigm shift for me was when I started doing that and having peace in the storm. The absolute difference between a believer and a non-believer is someone who can stay calm in the crisis, know God is in control, and thank him for the challenge. It's the most difficult and most rewarding way to pray.

PRAYER PARTNERS

It's not an absolute necessity, but if you are able to have a brother or sister in Christ as a prayer partner, that would be a great asset. Like a workout partner, it is great for accountability to motivate each other to keep pushing towards goals. Plus, you can reach out to each other and lift each other up in prayer if you are having tough days or struggling in a specific area. Remember, when two or more pray together in his name, Jesus is there with you. It's even more powerful than praying on your own (see Mt 18:19–20). God also says that "iron sharpens iron" (Prv 27:17) and that "bad company corrupts good character" (1 Cor 15:33), so having strong, likeminded relationships is essential to strengthen faith. Even if the relationship does not approach that of a prayer partner, you need people in your life walking the same path.

HUMILITY, HUMILITY, HUMILITY

Humility is the gymnastics of prayer stamina. The skills of balance, precision, strength of prayer, and awe-inspiring results are all wrapped up in learning to pray humbly. One of the most powerful and most important ways to pray is to do so humbly. How we approach God in prayer is a needed reflection for us all. In Luke 18, when the Pharisee prayed, he boasted about his virtue and how thankful he was he wasn't doing all the bad things others were doing. When the tax collector prayed, he humbly admitted he was a sinner and asked for mercy. We are all sinners and we can do nothing without God. Recognizing this and understanding this for our prayer life brings a great maturity.

The more I can detach from human desires, the more I reach new levels of holiness. I find the greatest humility in understanding that every time we sin, it hurts Jesus. It lashes him again, puts the crown of thorns on his head, gives him a kiss of Judas's betrayal. My final moment of healing/freedom from sexual bondage came from when I humbly would have given literally anything I had, my own life even, to not offend or hurt my Lord. I cried out to God with this fact one night. I cried out the Scripture about cutting an arm off before sinning against him. The humility and purity of my heart at that point, through the grace and mercy from the struggle to overcome sexual sin, freed me. He heard my most humble prayer of my entire life, and he immediately answered me. In that humility, the enemy cannot exist. He is completely rendered powerless.

Pride is the toughest of all the deadly sins because it's so easy to commit without knowing you are doing it! For greater awareness in this area, I highly suggest praying the Litany of Humility daily. Meditating on Scriptures on pride and humility are helpful as well. Those can both be found with a simple online search.

WE MUST BE WILLING TO SACRIFICE
FOR OUR PRAYER INTENTIONS

This leads us to our next section and what goes hand in hand with prayer: *fasting.*

Often times you hear of athletes and professional body builders going on juice fasts or some sort of fast to clear all the junk out of their bodies. Again, we can draw the same parallel when we fast in our spiritual lives to clean out all the junk in our souls.

Fasting *with* prayer will create a *major* jump in the success of your prayers and progress. Prayer without fasting is like weights without cardio in physical training. Both are great training options on their own, but it is the combination of the two that makes for top athletes. Fasting with prayer has greatly sculpted my spirit, and many others I have trained. Fasting is where your spiritual muscles turn into that visible six-pack. Keep going and you could even have a Mark Wahlberg or Daniel Craig eight-pack!

A lot of people forget about fasting, but all Christians should consider incorporating it into their prayer lives often. Every pastor I know from every Christian denomination says that fasting is one of the most important and powerful modes of spiritual strengthening. However, people seem to forget to do it when they have a major prayer intention.

My prayers are much more powerful when I'm offering something up to God for that intention. Rather than just asking for something, I'm willing to sacrifice and give up what I love most for the love of God and my neighbor. It teaches me continued discipline of self-control, which is a great gift of the Holy Spirit. Of course, self-control is a major component of chastity. The stronger the spirit of self-control is in you, the easier your chastity will become. The more you can strengthen that gift through fasting, the easier it will become!

Now usually when I mention fasting, people immediately assume it is about food, and ask if they have to stop eating. However, fasting is much broader than that in an offering for God. When deciding what your fast will be, pray about it using the methods in the previous section and ask the Lord to show you what he wants you to fast from and he will . . . some way, somehow. The exact answer you get from him will have to do with who you are as a person as well as your specific personal relationship with God. Usually, whatever is hardest to give up is the answer. Maybe you love steak, or have a favorite TV show, etc. The more we enjoy something in our humanity, the more valuable it is that our hearts are willing to give it up for the Lord.

Sometimes, without realizing it, we even start to idolize something in our lives because we really care about it. It could be a pet, a boat, another person, or running marathons. Jesus says in the Bible that we must be willing to give up all earthly things. In fact, we may not be connected to *anything* above him (see Gn 22; Lk 14:33). Anything we are attached to and not willing to sacrifice for him blocks us from him. As I mentioned in an earlier chapter, it used to be an issue for me when I was in relationships. I would begin loving the person God gave me as much or more than God himself, and that was getting in the way of my relationship with God. I actually fasted from dating for a while until I was able to make sure that God is always number one and that I worship him alone, not who he gives me. I really had to remember the Scripture of Luke 14:26, "If anyone comes to me and does not hate father and mother, wife and children, brothers and sisters—yes, even their own life—such a person cannot be my disciple."

So the key when fasting is to offer up something meaningful that will draw you closer to our most holy and ever-living God. Giving up something that is easy to go without and not very important to you will have much less of an effect. Showing God that he comes first over even the most important worldly things in your life is the key to a powerful fast.

Hopefully, your goal for yourself through this continued journey is that when someone asks you, "What are you willing to give up for God?" you will answer, "What wouldn't I give up?"

To inspire you as you begin to incorporate fasting into your life, I have included some testimonies and stories below!

Fasting for Special Intentions

Nine years ago when I was deathly ill, I wasn't able to sleep for almost six months. That story is a whole book in itself for another time, but what my mom used to do is truly my favorite example of fasting. I needed sleep so desperately that there were nights that my mom would give up her sleep for me and offer it up with her prayer for me so I could get a night's sleep. The amazing thing is I wouldn't even know she would do this, but I would sleep maybe one night a week, and it would end up being the night she had secretly given up her sleep to God as a sacrifice so I would have some rest to help me heal. While fasting is a wonderful and beautiful sacrifice to God so that we become stronger in him, it's even more beautiful when it's done for someone else and not for your own spiritual strengthening.

Fasting From Food for Special Intentions

A pastor friend of mine fasted for at least three months straight while I was sick, eating only one meal a day and then drinking liquid protein shakes to get him through those months. It made me feel less alone and like people were carrying my cross with me. I wholeheartedly believe I wouldn't even be here today without prayer and fasting, both my own and that done for me by others.

Fasting With the Sole Intention of Drawing Closer to God

A friend of mine would do this regularly, and I found it so beautiful that it really inspired me to start fasting in a real way. My friend gave up his car for forty days as a sacrifice to the Lord. He loved that car. He was crazy about that car. I couldn't believe he had given it up for forty days. When he showed up one day to meet me, I realized he had taken his fast to an entirely different level. He was driving this old decrepit pickup truck. I started laughing hysterically when I went to get in the passenger seat. It smelled so bad because, apparently, he had to bomb the thing for bugs. It was an emergency truck owned by the church, and it really was something that no one should ever get in unless it truly was an emergency. That was the moment I truly got it. Through his fast, it witnessed to me the importance of God above all else. I realized that "things" should never actually matter to me. It's fine to have nice things, but we can't care about them. We can take care of them but there cannot be any attachment or true worth given to them.

Group Fasting

I was having dinner with one of my friends recently, a wonderful dedicated Christian woman. Her eleven-year-old daughter was a week out from having major surgery. She was saying how much she was praying for her but trying not to think about it since there was really nothing more she could do. So I asked her instinctively, "Well, what are you giving up for her surgery? What are you fasting from?" She looked at me and said, "Fasting, hmmm, I never thought about fasting." We started talking about it and she said, "Well, I don't really eat much anyways, and I don't really like food, so I don't understand how that would be such a sacrifice." I explained to her that fasting doesn't have to have anything to do with food necessarily. It's about making an offering to God to show him how important this is to you, something selfless, something disciplined, something to show you are willing to help carry the cross for your prayer intentions.

So I asked her to pray and let me know what God reveals to her. I told her that I was going to fast for her as well, and the other girl at lunch suggested that not only would she fast but she wanted to get her children involved. Her kids were aware of the upcoming surgery, were friends with the girl, and felt helpless. This gave them all the opportunity to do something to help their friend. She later called me to tell me that God told her to give up her makeup for a month—the singularly most difficult thing for her and most important worldly thing to her. I think the kids fasted from chocolate or other favorite candy. The surgery was a success, not only physically, but for everyone's spirits. I think it lifted her spirit to know that we cared that much about her and were willing to sacrifice something enjoyable to us so we could show her we care and share in her suffering.

I hope these examples were a great help for you. Remember, though, that learning to fast and doing it well takes time and practice, so don't start with a three-month fast or you may just get frustrated and quit. That's what the enemy wants, and the last thing God wants for you. Perhaps start with a week or maybe the forty days of the devotional in chapter 6. God will show you the way!

Chapter 5

KICKBOXING UNHEALTHY SOUL TIES AND GENERATIONAL BONDAGES

THIS chapter includes what may be both the most powerful and most obscure spiritual exercises in the entire book. It's something that often remains untaught to the general Christian public. However, I believe it to be one of the most important tools to learn in this life-changing journey, and I want to share it will all of you. When you are ready to include it as a major way to kickbox the enemy and triumph over sexual sin, it's here for you.

I have always had a fierce right roundhouse kick in my workouts, and now I have that same powerhouse kick for the spirit. It's the method to break "unhealthy soul ties" and "generational bondage." These are two different issues, but for me, the combination of them was the one-two punch God gave me to knock Satan out cold regarding sexual sin, Glory be to God. So, if you haven't knocked out the struggle yet through the other chapters, here is a major answer for the toughest cases. Remember and be encouraged that the toughest battles are the greatest testimonies and show the absolute miraculous power of God!

This crucial information was something that I considered and prayed on deeply before including. I pondered for a long time why so many Christians don't know about this and ultimately came to two conclusions. One: The enemy doesn't want you to have this wisdom in Christ because it equals freedom. And two: It's not their time yet. God is beautiful in the way he works with us as he brings us to new levels up the mountain of faith-filled enlightenment. This came to me in the time I needed it most, after prayerfully begging and fasting day in and day out for final victory; it came when I was ready for it. If, as you are reading, you are not ready for the step now, or ever, that's okay. Be sure it's not fear from the enemy trying to deter you and instead let the Holy Spirit guide you for timing on this. Work with a good spiritual director that has experience with this process. Receiving guidance in this area and reading additional sound books on the subject would be wise.

I am 100 percent positive that in my own personal journey I would not be free without being led by the spirit to books, Catholic priests, deacons, lifelong exorcists, and even Protestant pastors, who taught me everything I know about how to break soul ties and generational bondage. For me, it was my final step to freedom. Even after my break from sexual sin itself, I was still dealing with the spiritual elements that caused the sin in the first place. If you don't know what I'm referring to, I will share with you Paul's

statement in Ephesians 6:12: "For we are not contend-
ing against flesh and blood, but against the principalities,
against the powers, against the world rulers of this present
darkness, against the spiritual hosts of wickedness in the
heavenly places." So even though the Lord had given me
the power to resist sin, I was still suffering deeply from that
evil which refused to give up on me. I was still on the bat-
tleground with spiritually attached sexual evil trying to find
a way back into my life.

Deliverance was an answer to over two years of prayer,
fasting, and full commitment to the other steps in this
book. This was the missing step! It took this missing piece
of the puzzle to complete a beautiful picture of victory. For
me, I finally was able to achieve and finally realize what
Jesus meant when he said, "For my yoke is easy and my
burden is light" (Mt 11:28–30). Prior to my breaking soul
ties *and* generational bondage in this area, my yoke was
neither easy nor was it light. It was so difficult and so unbe-
lievably heavy. I'm not sure who said, "ignorance is bliss,"
but it definitely wasn't God. It was indeed the wisdom and
knowledge of these biblical truths that broke me out of that
dark prison and into running free with Jesus!

Now, this step may not be needed for everyone to break
free. Each individual is different. The issue holding you
back may have already been found and corrected in any
of the steps in chapters 1–5. In an earlier chapter, you may
already have *your* piece of the puzzle to superhero chastity
status. However, in my five years of experience working

with Christian leaders regarding this step, it has often been needed to fully break free from the sin itself, the temptation of the sin, or the spiritual bondage of that sin. However, this can also truly be three in one, and some people either cannot stop sinning or break the torturous temptation to that sin until they break these spiritual bondages. When they do, the temptation they experienced and the actual sinning they did ceases. This is what we call "deliverance" from a specific area of struggle. This is true freedom and peace in Christ.

It is my hope that the forty-day devotional which follows will also lead you closer to the Lord and his peace.

Chapter 6

FORTY-DAY DEVOTIONAL FOR PURITY

DAY 1: THE LIGHT

"*The light shines in the darkness, and the darkness has not overcome it*" (Jn 1:5).

"*And he said: 'Truly I tell you, unless you change and become like little children, you will never enter the kingdom of heaven'*" (Mt 18:3).

Think back to when you were a little child, before your innocence was taken from you...or before you gave it away. If you allow me, I will restore you to that innocence. I will restore one of the ways you will be able to feel closest to me . . . the way of purity, in imitation of my own. When I said that you must be like little children, I not only meant that you must fully rely on me and trust in me, but I meant you must have a pure heart like a child. I will take all the darkness that you experienced while not following me, and I will remember them no more. You will be made new and the Holy Spirit will fill all those areas of darkness with the brightest light. I will make my home in you and shine through you like never before.

Prayer

God restore the purity of my heart. Make my heart your heart. Take all the broken pieces and make something beautiful and new.

DAY 2: COURAGE

"Be strong and courageous. Do not be afraid or terrified because of them, for the L<small>ORD</small> *your God goes with you; he will never leave you nor forsake you" (Dt 31:6).*

"For God has not given us a spirit of timidity, but of power and love and discipline" (2 Tm 1:7).

As you begin this journey with me, take courage. I am walking with you every step and carrying you when you are weary. You know that I tell my followers, "Do not be afraid." Trust me. Remember, I am going before you and will fight for you.

Be encouraged that you have everything you need to be successful in becoming pure. I will give you the grace and strength you need daily until it becomes second nature to your mind, heart, and body. Once they are in tune with your spirit, there is no stopping you from basking in my glory.

Prayer

God, it has been so long since I've done things your way and I'm still afraid. It's so difficult and I feel like I'm climbing a mountain to get to you. Jesus, as scared as I am, I want to change, and I am ready. Make me all that you want me to be.

DAY 3: PLAN

"Then the Lord replied:
'Write down the revelation
and make it plain on tablets
so that a herald may run with it.
For the revelation awaits an appointed time;
it speaks of the end
and will not prove false.
Though it linger, wait for it;
it will certainly come
and will not delay'" (Hb 2:2–3).

Write down your vision for chastity and how it will affect your relationship with me, the living God, who loves you unconditionally. I dwell in each and every person. Write down how, through this journey, I will come to dwell brighter and stronger than ever before. How do you see your purity and your chastity becoming a part of who you are? How do you envision it affecting your level of peace and your joy? How do you want it to affect the relationships around you in a positive way?

Prayer

Lord, reveal your plan and vision for my journey.

DAY 4: WORTH

"Then Jesus told them this parable: 'Suppose one of you has a hundred sheep and loses one of them. Doesn't he leave the ninety-nine in the open country and go after the lost sheep until he finds it?'" (Lk 15:3).

Oh, my child, why do you think you are worth so little to me? You think the things that you have done are so ugly that you aren't worthy of coming into my presence. Oh, if you only understood how infinite my love is for you. I promised you that nothing could separate you from my love. Come back to me and let me show you a new song. Let me show you how much I love you and desire to have you as close as possible to me. All you have to do is turn back and ask forgiveness, and your sins are cast as far as the east is from the west. Let me renew your soul and rebuild your heart. Let me be your best friend and make you a new creation. Whenever you feel unworthy of my love, remember my promises to you.

Prayer

Lord help me to forgive myself for my past life. Help me to start new and seek your love and tender mercies. Let me see myself through your eyes.

DAY 5: THE HEART

"Above all else, guard your heart, for everything you do flows from it" (Prv 4:23).

"For out of the heart come evil thoughts—murder, adultery, sexual immorality, theft, false testimony, slander" (Mt 15:19).

Sexual sin begins in the heart, and when you have lust in your heart, then you have already committed adultery in my eyes. The same is true for chastity. When your heart longs to be pure and to have pure thoughts, your flesh and your thoughts will come into alignment.

It makes sense then that I also say to guard your heart above all else. The more your thoughts become pure the more you will be able to live the life that I called you to fulfill. Start with your heart. What do you want regarding your relationships? Do you want my will for your life or do you want what you want for yourself? The more you are able to examine this and to align your wants with my wants for your life, the closer you will draw near to me.

Prayer

God, only you can make me pure. Change me from the inside out.

DAY 6: CLAY

"He told them: 'Take nothing for the journey—no staff, no bag, no bread, no money, no extra shirt'" (Lk 9:3).

"He said, 'Can I not do with you, Israel, as this potter does?' declares the Lord. Like clay in the hand of the potter, so are you in my hand, Israel" (Jer 18:6).

This journey has to be you and me alone. Sometimes you cannot take others where you are going. A butterfly first goes into a cocoon to be prepared for what is coming. This is a time to be molded into something new. This is a time to allow me to shape your clay on the potter's wheel. I AM. I am the artist of all the beauty within the world. Trust me to make you what you are called to be, a pure and holy house of the Holy Spirit. As my son was the spotless victim so you could be made spotless through me.

Prayer

Do with me as you will Lord. There is no more beautiful creation than what you will and prune and purify in the fire. Put me on your potter's wheel and let it end in the pure beauty I had previously disfigured in sin. Only you can make me whole again. Only you can make me truly beautiful.

DAY 7: PATH

"Every branch in me that does not bear fruit, he takes away; and every branch that bears fruit, he prunes so that it may bear more fruit" (Jn 15:2).

In the foreground, I hope all things, love all things, bear all things. I have brought you back from darkness, and now I am setting you on a new trajectory, one that will shape the rest of your life if you stay the course. I have plans for you to bring you to new heights, to new depths, to new understanding. In your sin, you tried to separate yourself from me, but I am always here waiting for you, ready to welcome you. Nothing can ever break the bond between you and your creator, till the end of all time.

Prayer

Continue to do your work in me, oh Lord. Continue to build me into all I have been praying for—a holy temple for the Lord. A Holy sepulcher that will house the Holy Spirit and not desecrate that house or the house of others. You have always guided me and shielded me and will do so again, now that I am back on your path. Let me never try to separate myself from you.

DAY 8: YOURS

"I have found the one whom my soul loves" (Sg 3:4).

"Neither height nor depth, nor anything else in all creation, will be able to separate us from the love of God that is in Christ Jesus our Lord" (Rom 8:39).

My love for you cries from the very depths of my soul. You were created in our likeness and image. You were set upon a rock. A rock that could not bend, that could not be swayed. Here you are with me, to join me one day in heaven, but as for now, do your work on this earth so nothing can separate you from me. I was always calling to you, longing for you, and now I have you back. The tears of the oceans are my love for you even in your sin. Come back to me fully to heal you and protect you and free you from your life of sin.

Prayer

Lord, Jesus Christ, I'm so ready to be back in your arms fully. I see you never left me, never stopped longing for my love. I'm sorry I was away from you for so long. I'm here to stay. Do with me as you will.

DAY 9: FOCUS

"On that day you will realize that I am in my Father and you are in me, and I am in you" (Jn 14:20).

"But few things are needed—or indeed only one. Mary has chosen what is better, and it will not be taken away from her" (Lk 10:42).

I come alive when you come to me, when you come to me like a little child. When you rest at my feet like Mary, when you wash my feet with your hair, when you rest in me in adoration. These are the moments that I elevate you out of this bondage, out of this sin, and into freedom of mind, body, heart, and soul. Your spirit soars in my presence. True love with me is what I desire most for you.

Prayer

Jesus, make me live in joyful wonder for you, like a little child. As long as I put you first and keep my eyes fixed on you, all else will come through you. Help me to choose what is better, every moment of my day.

DAY 10: FAITH

"'You unbelieving and perverse generation,' Jesus replied, 'how long shall I stay with you? How long must I put up wth you? Bring the boy here to me'" (Mt 17:17).

"I do believe, help me overcome my unbelief!" (Mk 9:24).

Your very freedom depends on your very faith in me. Do you believe that I can do this for you? Do you believe that I can make you whole? As I have told you, it is your faith that will save you. It is the fasting to increase that faith as you detach from the world and surrender your will to me that you will see the miracles that I will do in your life. Do you trust me? Do you trust me to free you and to help you? Or are you trying to do this on your own? I am your maker and I will restore you. You will be free.

Prayer

Lord, I want to trust you more. Show me what to fast from so that I can increase my faith and allow you to release me from this wall we have between us. Jesus, I trust in you. Jesus, I trust in you. Jesus, I trust in you.

DAY 11: OVERSEER

"You keep track of all my sorrows. You have collected all my tears in your bottle. You have recorded each one in your book" *(Ps 56:8 NLT).*

My sun rises and sets on you. Many others have been where you are and battled this concupiscence. There is no one who I have not aided who wanted to live for me and with me, throwing away the lusts of this world. Your flesh is here but for a moment, but your souls shall live forever. United to your body will you be again but only once all things are made new. Only once all has passed and there will be no more pain, no more sorrow, no more rain on your face. I have kissed your tears.

Prayer

Lord, you count all my tears. I know you are with me on this journey and you will take me to new levels, and I must be patient. Give me the grace to be patient as you change my life. I know your latter will be better than the former.

DAY 12: FREEDOM

"Jesus replied, 'Very truly I tell you, everyone who sins is a slave to sin. Now a slave has no permanent place in the family, but a son belongs to it forever. So if the son sets you free, you will be free indeed'" (Jn 8:34–36).

You have been a slave for so long and now you are coming to a resting place in me that you have not experienced before. I have so many wonders to show you, so many places to take my sons and my daughters. Your slavery is going to be a thing of the past that you will never forget but will never have to endure again. I know that's hard for you to believe, but once this freedom comes for you, nothing will ever take it away, without your consent, for I so loved you that I made you free. The slave mentality is being removed from your mind, your heart, and will no longer be made manifest in your body. Come with me.

Prayer

Jesus, I was a slave for so long, I don't even know what it looks like to be free, but I believe it and I want it with every fiber of my free will. Make my will your will Lord. Make my heart your heart Lord. Renew my mind so I can be free, and be your true heir.

DAY 13: THE WAY

"Jesus answered, 'I am the way and the truth and the life. No one comes to the father, except through me'" (Jn 14:6).

"Watch and pray so that you will not fall into temptation. The spirit is willing, but the flesh is weak" (Mt 26:41).

I am the only way for you to get through this battle. I am the only way to lead you to the purity you so desire. The heart is willing but the flesh is weak. I make you strong in your weakness. I restore your soul. Nothing comes to you except through me. Trust in me and I will give you rest for your soul.

Prayer

Guide me, mold me, free me, I pray.

DAY 14: FRIENDSHIP

"Greater love has no one than this: to lay down one's life for one's friends" (Jn 15:13).

"I pray for them. I am not praying for the world, but for those you have given me, for they are yours" (Jn 17:9).

I give everything for you. I gave my only begotten son for you as a sacrifice for your sins, because I love you that much. Can you comprehend the depths of my love for you? I am infinite because my love is infinite. You have turned back to me and I rejoice in your willingness to fight for that love, to offer up your body to the Holy Spirit for healing, for renewal, for purity. I AM, I remind you. There is nothing I cannot and will not do for you, as you have seen through my precious son and joy, Jesus Christ. The spotless lamb has laid down his life for you to be able to overcome all sin. Meditate on that love and no sin can overcome you.

Prayer

Thank you for my life God, thank you for the sacrifice of your son to give me life. I can have this life abundantly and I will do all I am able, every day to love you with every fiber of my being.

DAY 15: FOOTSTEPS

"And surely I am with you always, to the very end of the age"
(Mt 28:20).

"If the world hates you, keep in mind that it hated me first"
(Jn 15:18).

There will be days where you will feel alone, isolated, abandoned. Remember, I too felt all of those things. Remember, I too was misunderstood and rejected by the world. But fear not. Just as I walked with the apostles, I walk with you.

Prayer

Lord, help me to be strong like you. Help me to carry my cross and walk towards freedom, only found in you. Not my will, but your will be done. As you prayed in the garden of Gethsemane, as so many were coming to rise against you, teach me to drink my father's cup. Teach me to live in the mind of the spirit and not of the flesh.

Thank you, Lord for this opportunity to walk with you on this journey of chastity. I can feel you smiling as my heart becomes your heart.

DAY 16: TRIALS

"Though he slay me, yet will I hope in him" (Job 13:15).

"About three in the afternoon Jesus cried out in a loud voice, 'Eli, Eli, lema sabachthani?' (which means 'My God, my God, why have you forsaken me?')" (Mt 27:46).

You are going to have hard days. You are going to have days where you want to give up, where you feel mad that your journey is so difficult. You will even have days where you will wonder if I have abandoned you.

Prayer

Be merciful, oh Lord. Show me the way and keep me from becoming ungrateful. When trials of this life are upon me, I know that I have to rely on you completely. You save me and give me a grateful heart. But my human mind soon forgets the pit from which you pulled me and I begin to be ungrateful. I want more, I expect more. Please keep my heart grateful, even in the tough times. Do not let me become despondent, my Lord and my God. Do not let me go astray. Keep me close. I don't want to do anything to hurt you, and I know even lustful thoughts or immodest dress hurt you. It's so difficult in the modern age to keep sight of what is right from wrong. Show me the way.

DAY 17: MARRIAGE MINDED

"So the Lord God caused a deep sleep to fall upon the man, and he slept; then he took one of his ribs and closed up the flesh at that place. The Lord God fashioned into a woman the rib which he had taken from the man, and brought her to the man. The man said, 'This is now bone of my bones, And flesh of my flesh; She shall be called Woman, Because she was taken out of Man'" (Gn 2:21–23).

Marriage is a perfect covenant that I have created for you. Everything I do is deliberate and intricate in plan.

When I created Eve from Adam's rib, I created it from *one* of his ribs to show you my will for your life. He had more ribs that I could have drawn from, but I created only one helpmate for him, not many.

Prayer

Dear God, help me to understand the fullness of your will for me in all my relationships. If it is your will, lead me to the person you created for me, who is already flesh of my flesh and bone of my bone. But God, please only do this when I am ready to do things your way—strong enough to fulfill that relationship through a marriage-minded love with respect and a pure heart for your will.

DAY 18: THE HOLINESS OF MARRIAGE

"For this reason a man shall leave his father and his mother, and be joined to his wife; and they shall become one flesh. And the man and his wife were both naked and were not ashamed" (Gn 2:24–25).

I also showed you my absolute power and blessing over holy matrimony when my son's first miracle to glorify me was turning water into wine during the celebration of marriage.

Prayer

Father God, lead me away from all distractions and all potential partners that are not to be my marriage partner. Give me wisdom and discernment on this matter. You have chosen the perfect spouse for me, so please keep me from using my own will to choose a partner. Let me wait for you to bring me the flesh of my flesh.

DAY 19: HOPE

"For in this hope we were saved. But hope that is seen is no hope at all. Who hopes for what they already have? But if we hope for what we do not yet have, we wait for it patiently" (Rom 8:24–25).

"Therefore keep watch, because you do not know the day or the hour" (Mt 25:13).

"But the seed on good soil stands for those with a noble and good heart, who hear the word, retain it, and by persevering produce a crop" (Lk 8:15).

Begin to think of yourself already as married and just waiting for your spouse to come home. As one or both of you are still being prepared for the Holy Covenant, this is the time to grow in me and become the best husband or wife you possibly can be.

Prayer

Jesus, help me to be more like you every day. Continue to grant me the grace to follow you and learn from you so that I can become the person you want me to be. Let people see you when they see me. This is the time you have given me to really become that gift. Teach me the lessons so that they bear fruit in me; in that way, I will be prepared when, if it is your will, the one whom I should marry comes. Though I know not the hour or the day, I want to be ready.

DAY 20: HOLY SPIRIT

"But the fruit of the Spirit is love, joy, peace, forbearance, kindness, goodness, faithfulness, gentleness and self-control. Against such things there is no law. Those who belong to Christ Jesus have crucified the flesh with its passions and desires" (Gal 5:22–24).

You must be willing to be filled with the gifts of the Holy Spirit to imitate my Son in his purity. The more love and joy you are filled with, the more you will be able to have self-control. It will become easier for you to resist any temptation that would hurt me, yourself, or your future spouse. The more love you have for yourself and others, the more you will be transformed from the inside out.

Prayer

Holy Spirit, please fill me up. Fill up all the emptiness that would cause me to go against what is best for God. Change me from the inside out. Help me to know I am so loved by the God almighty that I don't long for love that is not of you. Teach me to be patient and have self-control. Keep me focused as I work for your kingdom and wait for my perfect helpmate, ordained by you and you alone.

DAY 21: ARMOR

"Finally, be strong in the Lord and in his mighty power."
(Eph 6:10).

Just like a soldier would not walk onto the battlefield without his armor for protection, so should you put on my holy armor daily. Every day you walk into the world of temptation and distractions. There will be many snares to try to take you off course. Remember that I am with you and have given you all the tools you need to not only make it through the day but to remain unscathed and to arise victorious. You will triumph over anything that comes your way that is not of me. Make me your armor and you will not fail.

Prayer

Dear Lord, I choose now to put on the armor of God so that I may be able to stand against the deceits of the devil. I take up the shield of faith so that I can extinguish the fiery darts of all evil. Gird my loins with truth and put on my breastplate of righteousness. Prompt me to put on the sword of the Spirit every morning, which is your Word, and by all prayer and supplication, pray at all times in the Spirit. Lord, let me remember to do this every morning when I wake.

DAY 22: SIMPLICITY

"The Lord is my shepherd, I shall not want. He makes me lie down in green pastures, he leads me beside quiet waters, he refreshes my soul. He guides me along the right paths for his name's sake" (Ps 23:1-3).

With me, you lack nothing. I always give you everything you need, when you need it. Any thought you have or external influences that tell you differently are not of the truth. I will never lead you astray. The more you fill yourself with me, the less you will be searching outside yourself for something to bring you peace or joy. When your heart is ready to seek me in all things, I will bring you that earthly love as well.

Prayer

Father God, help me to want for nothing but you. I want to be so filled with your presence that the only thing I need is your love and all I have to give is from you. It will make me a better partner for the person you have prepared for me. As I am patiently waiting, I will always remember all good comes from you. I will seek only you and praise only you.

DAY 23: POWER

"For if you live according to the flesh, you will die; but if by the Spirit you put to death the misdeeds of the body, you will live" (Rom 8:13).

"But he said to me, 'My grace is sufficient for you, for my power is made perfect in weakness.' Therefore I will boast all the more gladly about my weaknesses, so that Christ's power may rest on me" (2 Cor 12:9).

There will be days when you feel like you cannot win the battle over your body, but keep fighting. The day will arrive like it has for so many where it won't be a battle anymore. There will be a time when your spirit is healed such that that which torments you now will no longer do so.

Prayer

Father, Son, and Holy Spirit, give me strength to make it to the finish line. I know I will always have to be careful and as a human being, I'm always going to be subject to sin. But I also know that if I keep fighting, I will be on the winning side of the battle, the downslope of this mountain.

DAY 24: BELIEVE

"He answered, 'A wicked and adulterous generation asks for a sign but none will be given it except the sign of the prophet Jonah'" (Mt 12:39).

"And he said to them, 'This kind cannot be driven out by anything but prayer'" (Mk 9:29).

Believe in me. Believe in the one who made you and who called you to have life and have it more abundantly. Believe in the one who was sent to you to heal you of your infirmity. I can do no work or only partial work without your belief and participation in your healing. I will give you the grace; will you cooperate with me? Walk with me and trust me. I AM the Lord, your God.

Prayer

Lord, help me to believe in you. Help me to have faith like a mustard seed, God. You said the mustard seed was the smallest of all seeds, but grew up to be the biggest tree, so big that birds could perch on its branches. Make me that tree Lord!

As I meditate on your truths, please show me what to offer up in fasting. I want to unite my fast to my prayer petitions for purity.

DAY 25: FULFILLMENT

"Come to me all who are weary and burdened, and I will give you rest" (Mt 11:28).

"Ask and it will be given to you; seek and you will find; knock and the door will be opened to you. For everyone who asks receives; the one who seeks, finds; and to the one who knocks, the door will be opened." (Mt 7:7–12).

I am all that you need. All life flows from me and through me. Come to me and let me make your crooked ways straight. You are spending time looking for love in so many empty places. You are searching and searching but only with me will you find. So ask, seek, knock, and your freedom will be given to you.

Prayer

God, give me a greater understanding of your love for me. Let me feel your love in new ways. Please remove all blocks, in Jesus's name, that are creating a wall between me and your loving peace.

DAY 26: SURRENDER

"I am the vine; you are the branches. If you remain in me and I in you, you will bear much fruit; apart from me you can do nothing" (Jn 15:5).

"Every branch in me that does not bear fruit, he takes away; and every branch that bears fruit he prunes so that it may bear more fruit." (Jn 15:2).

Remember this war cannot be won without me. If you try to do this in your own will, it cannot work because the enemy is stronger than humanity, yet I am stronger than anything or anyone. The more you invite me into your heart and mind, the more you will be able to overcome the enemy and win this final battle. Know that I am the Lord your God, and I will remove this evil from you.

Prayer

Jesus, I know I can do nothing of value without you. The rest is loss. There was so much loss, so much that needed to be pruned and changed in me. I see you doing a great work in me. Thank you, God! Help me to keep going.

DAY 27: TRUST

"For now we see only a reflection in a mirror; then we shall see face to face. Now I know in part, then I shall know fully, even as I am fully known" (1 Cor 13:12).

Trusting in me is the surest way to salvation. A good father will lead you in the very best ways for your immortal soul. Is there anything I wouldn't do for you? I know there have been things that have happened to you which make you doubt my love for you. There is no end to the ways in which I protect and guard you, but there are also the effects of sin (your own sins and the sins of others), which I have not ordained, but have allowed. It is those times I weep with you and lift you up, shining my light into those times of darkness. I know you want to know why I don't just end it, but when you are with me in heaven, I will share with you that mystery and all truth.

Prayer

Lord help me to have peace in my mind, soul, and heart. I want to trust you more. Please remove any and all doubts about your goodness and your power to heal me. There is nothing you can't do. Help me to believe that and remove all worry, doubt and anxiety.

DAY 28: VANTAGE POINT

"Then Jesus laid his hands on his eyes again; and he opened his eyes, his sight was restored, and he saw everything clearly" *(Mk 8:25).*

I want to show you a new way to see. I want you to see every person with utmost value and worth, the worth that I was willing to die for. If I was willing to hang on a tree to break the curse for your very souls, then how must I look at you, at each human person. Their dignity and value overwhelm me with joy, and I want you to feel that joy towards each of them. Take off your eyes of the flesh and put on those of my Spirit. Revel in the creations I have made, not for your fleshly pleasure and use, but as a little one of God. Cherish each person's authentic pure beauty that is not to be defiled but celebrated with the purest of love.

Prayer

Jesus, help me to see each person through your eyes and not my own. Make my eyes your eyes Lord. Help me to see each person as your child, and let me value them the way that you do. Love them through me Jesus.

DAY 29: REBUILDING

"And he who was seated on the throne said, 'Behold, I am making all things new'" (Rv 21:5).

"Though your sins are like scarlet, they shall be as white as snow" (Is 1:18).

Through this struggle, I know you have been broken down, but now I come to restore you. I come to give you life everlasting. There is nothing that is impossible through me, and now it is time for a new dawn. I love you beyond all measure, beyond your human understanding, and yet, still you doubt that love and forgiveness. Ask for my strength, to know that I love you equally in your sin and in your struggle. This is where my grace abounds even more. This is where I can come in and release you from these shackles and chains.

Prayer

I'm sorry God. I want to accept your merciful forgiveness. It's my pride and fear that keeps me from accepting it and forgiving myself. I believe you make me a new creation and white as snow. Help me to leave the past in the past and have a new, better life, with you. I love you Lord.

DAY 30: FUTURE

"I have come that they may have life and that they may have it more abundantly" (Jn 10:10).

"Let me hear joy and gladness. Let the bones that you have crushed rejoice" (Ps 51:8).

"Flesh gives birth to flesh, but the Spirit gives birth to spirit" (Jn 3:6).

Each year with me will become more abundant in the richness and fullness of my love. I know the suffering that you have endured in this trial. I know the pain it has caused you, and the torment it has caused your soul. I have come to lead you out of flesh and into glory. I will never lead you astray. As you continue to abandon the ways of the flesh and take on those of my Holy Spirit, the transformation will bring the joy and peace you have longed for.

Prayer

It's hard for me to believe that you have all these wonderful things in store for me. In my suffering, I struggle to know what good will be in my future, but I believe in your promises and I stay steadfast awaiting their fulfillment.

DAY 31: PLANS

"For I know the plans I have for you,' declares the LORD, *'plans to prosper you and not to harm you, plans to give you hope and a future'"* (Jer 29:11).

This too shall pass. All things are changing but I never change. I am working with you towards your freedom. I have never stopped loving you and have never abandoned you. I have always been at your side, except for those times when I have gone ahead of you into battle on your behalf. The time has come now. The time has come for a newfound freedom. Will you accept this freedom and walk in new ways with me? I have so much more I want to give and show you. Are you ready?

Prayer

Lord, my God, I want to be ready. I want to receive the fullness of what you have for me. I still feel like I'm struggling, but I already see the changes you have wrought in my life and the freedom you have granted me . . . and I trust that there is more to come. I will not doubt you Lord. Even when the waters are rising around me, I know you will rescue me. I'm ready Lord.

DAY 32: FREEDOM

"So if the Son sets you free, you will be free indeed" (Jn 8:36).

"When Jesus saw their faith, he said to the paralyzed man, 'Son, your sins are forgiven'" (Mk 2:5).

So many have been praying for you, here in heaven and on earth. I have laid your name on the hearts and lips of the faithful to pray for you, more than you even know. There is nothing you have done that can keep us apart or make me not love you. Those lies of the enemy that you tell yourself . . . they hinder your freedom but my love has never and will never leave you. With me, you stand upon a rock foundation that cannot be moved. All you have to do is stand, stand in my truth, and I will do the rest.

Prayer

Jesus, I'm ready now. I'm ready for this victory and can see the light ahead. All that I have is yours. Make me clean. Make me new Lord. I'm ready to close all doors where the enemy has had me in bondage. Make me anew.

DAY 33: RESTORATION

"[Jesus] said to the man, 'Stretch out your hand.' He stretched it out, and his hand was completely restored" (Mk 3:5).

I made those hands. I created every finger and every line. I want those hands to be used for doing good, not evil. I want to bless your hands and bless their work. Can you feel me anointing the purity of your hands so that they become clean and new hands, hands to do the innocent work of the Lord? I washed the feet of my disciples to cleanse them for holiness. I wash away sin through your baptismal vows. Renew those vows and renew your covenant with me.

Prayer

I make the commitment today to renew my baptismal vows.

(Note: Baptismal vows of both the Latin and English rite may be found online with a quick search. I recommend reviewing and considering both.)

DAY 34: MODESTY

"Instead, make up your mind not to put any stumbling block or obstacle in the way of a brother or sister" (Rom 14:13).

"Therefore, as God's chosen people, holy and dearly loved, clothe yourselves with compassion, kindness, humility, gentleness and patience" (Col 3:12).

Your body is the house of the Holy Spirit. Let it be adorned accordingly. Let it not be used for lustful thoughts and stumbling blocks but for its highest and noblest use, as a welcome home and dwelling place for my Spirit. While what you wear with a pure heart is pleasing to me, when you adorn yourself so as not to be a stumbling block to your brother and sister in their walk, it is even more pleasing to me. Let it be a testament to your faith and your purity. As you understand your value in me, understand your body is as precious as the Ark of my Covenant. It is good to cover such power the Lord has given. Shield that power, knowing that your body is good, and thus, take care of it in the ways of modesty now.

Prayer

Lord, I've been told for so long my value was based on the outside, so I thought that my body was what I was supposed to focus on and show the world.. Thank you for opening my eyes to be what you have called me to be: a holy vessel of you.

DAY 35: HUMILITY

"Humble yourselves, therefore, under God's mighty hand, that he may lift you up in due time" (1 Pt 5:6).

There is so much to humility that my people do not understand. It's about coming to me lovingly, trustfully, unattached to all things and people of this world. The more this is possible in a life, the more I can do with that life and the more I can do through that soul. Look unto me, little one, for your path to salvation.

Prayer

"Litany of Humility"

Oh Jesus, meek and humble of heart, hear me.
From the desire of being esteemed, deliver me Jesus
From the desire of being loved, deliver me Jesus.
From the desire of being extolled, deliver me Jesus.
From the desire of being honored, deliver me Jesus
From the desire of being praised, deliver me Jesus.
From the desire of being preferred to others, deliver me
    Jesus.
From the desire of being consulted, deliver me Jesus.
From the desire of approved, deliver me Jesus.
From the fear of being humiliated, deliver me Jesus.
From the fear of being despised, deliver me Jesus.
From the fear of suffering rebukes, deliver me Jesus.
From the fear of being calumniated, deliver me Jesus.
From the fear of being forgotten, deliver me Jesus.

From the fear of being ridiculed, deliver me Jesus.

From the fear of being wronged, deliver me Jesus.

From the fear of being suspected, deliver me Jesus.

That others may be loved more than I, Jesus grant me the grace to desire it.

That others may be esteemed more than I, Jesus grant me the grace to desire it.

That in the opinion of the world, others may increase and I may decrease, Jesus grant me the grace to desire it.

That others may be chosen and I set aside, Jesus grant me the grace to desire it.

That others may be praised and I unnoticed, Jesus grant me the grace to desire it.

That others may be preferred to me in everything, Jesus grant me the grace to desire it.

That others may become holier than I, provided that I may become as holy as I should, Jesus grant me the grace to desire it.

DAY 36: UNION

"But he was pierced for our transgressions; he was crushed for our iniquities; upon him was the chastisement that brought us peace, and with his wounds we are healed" (Is 53:5).

Sometimes you will feel like you are alone in this battle. Know that many are battling with you and for you. I never leave a little one alone. I always come to the aid of those who need me. Call out to me in your times of trouble and let me fill you with my strength and power to overcome this thorn in your flesh. Right now, I give you grace to endure the pain and hard times, but the day will come when I will remove this chalice from you. But remember to always unite your suffering to my own.

Prayer

I do cry out to you God. I need your help. Give me strength to bear this suffering Lord and please take it from me. But not my will, your will be done. I know you are working on me for my ultimate freedom from this bondage. I know you will remove this from me. I trust it has already been done. I offer up this suffering in union with Jesus Christ, in his passion, for freedom from all sexual sin.

DAY 37: CONQUER

"In all these things, we are more than conquerors through him who loved us. For I am convinced that neither death or life, neither angels nor demons, neither the present nor the future, nor any powers, neither height nor depth, nor anything else in all creation, will be able to separate us from the love of God, that is in Christ Jesus our Lord" (Rom 8:37–39).

If you could only see yourself through my eyes and know who you are and whose you are. You are a beautiful creation that has been made by me. I have made you a masterpiece and you are beautiful in my eyes. There is nothing that cannot be redeemed when you come into my arms. There is nothing that cannot be healed and there is nothing that can separate you from my love.

Prayer

God, let me see myself through your eyes. Let me heal from all my past mistakes and sin. Let me no longer live in darkness.

DAY 38: LOVE

"Let all that you do be done in love" (1 Cor 16:14).

"Do nothing out of selfish ambition or vain conceit. Rather, in humility value others above yourselves" (Phil 2:3).

I want you to do everything out of love. To understand this fully, stay in my word. The world doesn't understand love because they do not know me. But you have sought my face. You have found me and are on the path to everlasting life. Stay rooted in my word. Let no selfish deceit lead you astray. There is great love where I am taking you, love you are not used to because of your past. Now that you are with me and my Spirit is guiding you, there is an abundance of love waiting for you both here on earth and for eternity with me in heaven. Stay steady. Stay focused. Stay diligent.

Prayer

Lord keep my eyes fixed on you. Let nothing distract me from who you have called me to be and what you have called me to do. Let your wisdom press upon my heart as I walk in your ways.

DAY 39: HONOR

"You were bought at a price. Therefore, honor God with your bodies" (1 Cor 6:20).

"For you have been called to live in freedom, my brothers and sisters. But don't use your freedom to satisfy your sinful nature. Instead, use your freedom to serve one another in love" (Gal 5:13).

You were bought for a price. The price of my son, who was tortured and crucified for your redemption and salvation. Knowing this, what wouldn't you give up for that kind of love? And yet, what more will you gain?

Prayer

Jesus, help me to honor you with my body. I don't want to hurt you Jesus, or anyone else. I understand sexual sin and even the lust in my mind and heart hurts myself, others, and most of all you, who I want to love with everything I am. Please give me the grace to overcome fully. Please give me the mercy to know if I stumble still on that path to freedom, I can immediately start again through confessing my sins, doing penance, and continuing to amend my life.

DAY 40: LOVED

"For God so loved the world that he gave his one and only son, that whoever believes in him shall not perish but have eternal life" (Jn 3:16).

"For we are God's masterpiece. He has created us anew in Christ Jesus, so we can do the good things he planned for us long ago" (Eph 2:10 NLT).

I love you. Do you hear me? I love you. I love you. I love you.

Prayer

I finally get it God. I finally am able to begin to accept your love for me. Thank you, God, for loving me. Thank you for giving me life. Thank you for your forgiveness and this redemption. Help me to forgive myself for my past and know I am truly a new creation in you. I am ready to sing a new song.

Chapter 7

DAILY VITAMINS: THE CHURCH

THE ONE STOP SHOP

WHEN I wrote every other chapter in this book, with the exception of half of the devotional, it was three or four years ago, and I was trying to write something ecumenical that could be read and used by all Christian denominations, without including any areas where theological differences would keep any Christian from reading. After I completed the book, I sent out sample chapters to various publishers and received some offers to release the book. However, the Holy Spirit made sure I did not accept any of those deals. God pressed on my heart to put the book aside and patiently await the right publisher and his timing. Sure enough, he came through and here we are.

In hindsight, I can see why the timing is now and not then. From a human perspective, I thought two years ago, "But people need help *now*." However, as I write this, I realize that I wasn't ready a few years ago. While giving an ecumenical book would be helpful, it wouldn't be the fullness of the help, and while it was the truth, it wasn't the fullness of the truth. It took me a few years to realize that while the previous book version was for everyone struggling with sexual sin, I was holding back some of the keys to the purity kingdom that could potentially make all the difference in a soul's journey to chastity.

VITAMINS, SUPER FOODS, AND SPIRITUAL TRAINERS

When on a regular exercise regime, it's fairly imperative to take vitamins. Many of us go to specialized vitamin stores to really make our workouts count as well as to keep a steady overall health consistency. Vitamins allow us to supplement things we aren't getting in our daily lives, or that we need additional amounts of than we would otherwise consume daily. For example, if I'm feeling really run down, 1000 mg of vitamin C is much needed to get through the day. If I miss my organic multivitamin, I definitely have less energy and feel less equipped not only for my workouts but for the daily grind of life. Are you able to work out without the vitamins? Probably. Are you able to reach the athlete champion status without them? Maybe. Or maybe not.

I consumed very specific and certain vitamins, ate superfoods that boosted my health, strength, and energy, and worked with very specific personal trainers throughout my journey to chastity. If I didn't tell you about them, then I would be leaving out one important piece of my daily regimen, one crucial part of that which brought me freedom. I would be leaving you at a disadvantage if I didn't share the center piece to the spiritual eight-pack.

VITAMINS OF LOVE

Now, at the beginning of this book, I shared that everything starts with love. God's love for us and us loving him back. And yet even with that reciprocal relationship, Christ loving us is not dependent on us loving him back. He loves us no matter what.

I bring this up because, as I write this, I'm physically sitting in a very special place of a very powerful superfood, a place where I feel Jesus is able to show me such an immense amount of love that words can't fully express. If I don't share the location I have been going since I discovered this place years ago, where they have been cultivating this superfood for thousands of years, well, I don't think I would be doing right by you, myself, or God.

When I first wrote this book, I was ecumenical in all things Jesus. As long as Jesus was the center, as he is working the miracles, then that is what I believed everyone needed. Now, as I look in the rearview mirror years after my healing, I honestly don't know if I could say I would have been healed without this. It is a very special place where Jesus resides and loves us, with all that he is. It is the holy Catholic Church.

While it was the Protestant Church that started my awakening to Jesus Christ and that relationship with Christ that led me to desire purity and chastity, it was after my

Catholic conversion that I was actually able to achieve that desire. I wasn't in a vacuum, so I don't know if all of the other steps over time would have worked without the Catholic faith. As I search my heart of hearts, I know the answer, for my journey, is no.

With hindsight, I know that I simply do not believe I could have been completely freed from sexual sin without what I will describe in this chapter, one more conclusive chapter that I must share. One more truth, in black and white, full of powerful tools for your spiritual arsenal. This is about the training ground for spiritual warriors: the Church, the Holy Catholic Church.

While I will always recognize the power of all "church" in general, of all Christians gathering in his name—the biblical truth of "when two or more pray, there I am between you", with "three or more a cord cannot be broken" and "anything that you agree upon in my name that will I do for you"—there is so much more the Lord has offered us through that "church" that has been with us for two thousand years, originating from Jesus himself in that last supper, and then passed down through the apostles.

THE POWER OF THE EUCHARIST

Now I can easily say being Catholic is one of the best things that has ever happened to me. This subsection is my number one reason (of many reasons) why. In my conversion to devout Catholic practice, I was specifically healed many times over by the Eucharist. Having a realization that the

Eucharist truly was the body and blood of Christ is probably one of the most transformative events in my life. A
life-threatening illness early in my Catholicism proved to
me that the Eucharist was indeed Jesus's flesh and blood.
A priest would bring me daily Communion, and right after
I would consume the Host (Jesus under the appearance of
bread), it was the only time of the day I would feel well or
have strength or peace in a very marked difference. Once
this awakening happened, I literally spent almost every
day forward taking Communion daily, and once I was well
enough, going to daily Mass and adoration. Uniting with
Jesus in the Eucharist cannot even be compared to a vitamin though, as it's more like a miracle-causing super food!
To the outside world, I best compare it to Popeye's spinach. Every time I am able to take the Eucharist as food, my
spiritual muscles are bursting at the seams! I also notice a
decline in my spiritual strength if I miss a day. If I miss
more than a day, my ability to overcome sin noticeably
diminishes. To leave out this "super food" and all of its
benefits would not be fair to you. I'm not saying you can't
find your purity health without the Eucharist. It is true that
Jesus is Jesus and he does miracles in his name. However, in
my heart of hearts, I don't believe I would be living free of
sexual sin, and with ease, without the Eucharist.

Jesus Christ gave himself up for us and offers himself to
us in the Eucharist through the process of transubstantiation. Did you know that every time there is a Mass, we defy
all space and time and go back two thousand years to the

original sacrifice of Jesus on the cross to share in his passion and reflect on the unparalleled love offered up to us? Yes, every single day! I know many can't believe there is church not only on Wednesdays and Sundays but every day of the week. Multiple times a day the Mass is celebrated for us to unite with him and receive this unbelievable power. Jesus comes there in the flesh, in a mystery. He allows us to take him into our bodies to gain grace and strength and all the gifts of the Holy Spirit. We have him right there every day and so many of us take that for granted and don't even go on Sundays to receive his healing power. We are so lucky in the United States, as in some countries Catholic practice is restricted or they have to hide underground. I would be willing to die to get to the Eucharist. Once you know the love and sacrifice that is there, you will do whatever it takes to go as much as possible to unite with Jesus in that way. I fell in love, madly in love.

But wait, there's more!

As we partake of Christ's life through the Eucharist, we can also commune with our Lord through a devotion called Eucharistic Adoration. I find that many people, even many Catholics, aren't aware of this wonder of the world. The adoration chapel, that place where the Eucharist is reserved and displayed, is a place where we can go and hang out with Jesus like we would go to dinner with a best friend or to the beach together. And if you are in love, don't you want to spend as much time as possible with your beloved? You go to adoration at church or in a chapel and sit with him, conversing quietly. There's no church service or talking, sometimes there is music, but it's just you and him. You can talk with him, cry with him, giggle with him, fight with him if you have to.

I personally go to an adoration chapel every Friday night and have date night with him. That is a wonderful time in your singleness to enjoy and help you along your journey.

So many days and nights . . . for a few years every day or night (some churches offer this twenty-four hours!), I would go to be with him and ask him for the freedom I now have. I once heard an amazing saying that went something like "what you are living today is answered prayers from years ago." It most certainly is.

Remember with God, "today is a thousand years and a thousand years is a day." When a prayer seems like it may not be answered, it may be still to come. Consider making a commitment to go to Mass more than Sundays and ask the Lord in front of the Blessed Sacrament to free you. Ask him every day in his Eucharistic presence until he completes your miracle.

There is no sweeter time than being alone with Jesus, and there is nothing more precious than the time spent with him when we are in the greatest pain and greatest need. It's the only time we cannot, in any way, depend on ourselves. It's the only time we have to give everything to him, for him, trusting him completely to deliver us. And also letting him know that if he doesn't do what we have asked, even begged, if Jesus doesn't "come through" for our greatest prayer, that it's okay and we love him anyways. We still want to be with him and long for him. That is true love, right?

A ROSARY A DAY KEEPS THE ENEMY AT BAY

Mary, Our Lady of Perpetual Help, as I love to call her, is a powerhouse of all powerhouses. If you want a workout drink to boost your spiritual power, then do a daily Rosary.

Our Lady came to help me early on in my journey to Catholicism. I'm sure she was also there with me before I even realized it. The first time I tried to do a Rosary (which, for the record, is part of Luke 2 in Scripture), I guessed I was supposed to pray a Hail Mary prayer on every bead. She didn't care. She still showed up to help just knowing I was trying.

It is unfortunate that Mary, Christ's own mother, is difficult for so many to accept and embrace; it's unfortunate because she is so amazingly powerful against Satan. His demons are no match for her. Why is that? I've pondered this for a long time, and ultimately, I think it comes down to humility. As God is love, Satan literally is pride. There would be nothing worse than being overpowered by a little woman, and a human being at that. The demons are so envious of humans because we take their place in heaven and we are supposed to be "lesser" creatures than the angels. So what could be worse from their perspective than a human who was the epitome of obedience and humility to God, the exact opposite of everything that Satan is. It makes perfect sense if we think about it.

I, and many others I have known, are personal testimonies to the power of using the daily Rosary. Praying it as part of our daily regimen has elevated our spiritual fortitude to enable us to break out of sexual sin and become better followers of Christ. I know that many Protestants think or say Catholics pray to Mary, but in actuality, we ask her to pray for us. The most powerful prayers would come from the mother of our Lord.

I share this truth because I believe endless Rosaries helped me with all I went through, not only in that feminine mystique of power, but in the very nature of comfort. A mother's nature is to comfort. We all need that in our brokenness in this fallen world in order to heal and to thrive. Having a mother to watch over us and pray that the Father hears us and answers us is often a mother's job. Furthermore, in the book of Esther, Esther, though in an inferior position to the king, was able to persuade the king with that feminine mystique to save all the Jews. When we need help and saving in dire circumstances, Mary is most certainly a trusted source who will aid us and fight for us in our requests to God!

Our Lady of Perpetual Help, come to all reading this to ask God they be freed from all sexual sin and overcome all temptations. Amen.

THE SAINTS

Oh wow. Talk about getting amazing spiritual trainers, and for free. They aren't just an hour a week with a high price tag on them to help motivate you in your workouts. No, we're talking free workout coaches anytime I called on their names. I couldn't believe it. When Padre Pio first started coming to me in all different ways, I had no idea who he even was. Come to find out, St. Padre Pio had the stigmata for over thirty years in his hands and feet and tried to hide it. He had so many amazing spiritual gifts of healing, discernment of spirits, and even bilocation! The first time Pio revealed himself to me, I was really sick during a private Mass being given for my healing, and I laid down at the edge of the pew and the gold plaque for that row was dedicated St. Pio. Another time I was at Mass and there was a Padre Pio devotional and prayer booklet on the empty seat directly in front of me. I asked everyone if it was theirs, but no one knew where it had come from. I have it to this very day. Once I started reading about Padre Pio's life and asking for his intercession, he started teaching me. He taught me and sent priests to teach me spiritual warfare. He taught me how to fight Satan with spiritual means. I could feel him when I called for his help in times of distress, and he interceded for me against the enemy's attacks.

St. Philomena: A super powerful saint, and specific patron of purity, and one that I believe wholeheartedly interceded for my final freedom. St. Philomena is the ultimate intercessor for chastity because of all she went through in her short life. There isn't much known about her life, but after they found her bones, miracles started to occur. Then a nun claimed that St. Philomena came to her and told her about her life. She was martyred for her purity and chastity, which she had vowed at age thirteen.

As a young teenager, the emperor targeted her to be his wife, but she resisted fully. For this, she was scourged and then thrown in the ocean tied to an anchor, but angels came to her aid to heal and save her. Then he tried to have her burned, but she was again healed and protected by angels. St. Philomena was such a brave tiny girl that she stood up to the emperor, willing to die for her purity. Ultimately, she was martyred when the emperor succeeded in his murderous attempts by decapitating her. But he didn't win, because she kept her chastity till death and still assists many souls around the world with spiritual protection from sexual sin.

During the time of my struggle with my addiction, wearing St. Philomena's rope around my waist was a huge deterrent for the enemy. However, it was her holy oil that most decisively brought her intercession. I literally was praying for her intercession and secretly wearing her rope under my clothes when a priest came to me with St. Philomena's oil to pray over me during deliverance, and I got a *huge* healing that day. You can order her oil and chastity rope (it's thin and white, made out of red and white string, nothing scary) online, and I highly recommend you let her help you on this journey to freedom. She is your faithful friend and will not disappoint.

St. Gemma Galgani: St. Gemma is an Italian saint that suffered so much from continued illnesses throughout her life, but especially from spiritual bondage. She would levitate on Fridays at 3 p.m. to share in Jesus's passion. She is a powerful intercessor, and I took her name for my confirmation saint. It was both her and Padre Pio that were my closest friends in heaven, but when I had to pick one, Padre Pio was so humble, he acquiesced. Asking her to pray for me during that time, I found to be extremely powerful and comforting.

There are so many other amazing saints in history to learn about and ask for prayers from. However, what I love most is that I have found that the ones that your intentions fit most with will find their way to you. Someone will mention it, you will see something about them, or you will hear that it is their feast day and feel extra excited about that day. Enjoy and utilize your discovery!

SACRAMENT OF RECONCILIATION

In my earlier chapter on forgiveness, I shared the importance and biblical reference to confessing your sin to another. If I left it at that, I wouldn't be giving you the fullness of what the Lord has to offer. In the Catholic faith, we get the beautiful sacrament of confession. I personally go to confession once a week. I pray more people would take advantage of it. It's an amazing opportunity to ensure staying in a state of grace. It is also, when you have a good confessor, an amazing way to grow in virtue and humility.

Instead of just going in and reciting your number of sins and list of sins, go in with a heart rooted in and formed by the "act of contrition" we say at the end of each confession. Confession is three parts: confessing sins, doing penance, and amending the life. It's a beautiful opportunity to learn more about ourselves and grow in holiness, which is our goal overall.

Regarding sexual sin, I know when you are in that addiction, it is very difficult to go to confession. It gets so frustrating to keep going back again and again for the same sin, and it can be embarrassing if it is the same priest that you confessed it to a week before. Remember how important humility is! This is all part of the process of allowing God to work and seeing we are trying our best and we want to be out of sin. God sees this and he gives great graces and blessings for it. We can't quit or give up; we definitely must go and should not be ashamed. Shame is a major tactic of the enemy to keep us from getting free. Also, remember in the previous chapter on forgiveness that "the prayer of a righteous person is powerful and effective" (Jas 5:16). It is very powerful to have a priest praying for you to obtain that freedom and to move that darkness into the light, where it cannot live.

SPIRITUAL WARFARE ARSENAL

While other denominations are aware of and know to engage in spiritual warfare, Catholics have the most tools in the arsenal. I personally want all the tools I can possibly get to fight against Satan. I will take the Holy Trinity and the sacraments and Eucharistic Adoration and the holy saints and their holy relics and warfare prayers and blessed oil, blessed salt, and holy water. I will consecrate my house to the Sacred Heart of Jesus and the Immaculate Heart of Mary. And on and on goes the list of things I put in our spiritual warfare arsenal. The arsenal of Jesus's Church is serious business. All of these tools will help you in your quest for purity.

SUFFERING

In workouts, the saying often goes, "no pain, no gain." I wholeheartedly believe this is true for the spiritual life as well. This is one of the main reasons I knew the Catholic Church was the one true Church. It's the only one that understands and gives a full theological explanation for suffering. The Catholic Church shares the meaning of suffering and the value in it. Thousands of years of saints suffered the greatest to do the absolute most good in the world for others and to have their souls purified for heaven.

A dear friend of mine worked with Mother Angelica for over twenty years. He said that after she had her miraculous EWTN healing, and the braces fell off her legs, she told him she actually missed the suffering. She shared with my friend that she missed having that level of suffering to offer up to the Lord. I understand her. The greatest suffering seems to be the most powerful prayers, allowing me to witness many miracles, like the miracles of my own conversion and those of so many other souls.

As humans, we don't want to suffer. We, in our flesh, want everything to be good and many want things easy, but this is not Jesus's way. Jesus told his disciples that if they followed him, they would have to pick up their cross and suffer. So if we want to look like Christ and his followers, we must suffer to attain that final resting place of heavenly bliss.

Might I offer a wonderful exercise shared with me by a spiritual director. I was told to take that suffering and offer it up "in union with Jesus's passion." This is especially powerful if you do it during Mass, right after your priest lifts up the chalice of blood during transubstantiation.

EMOTIONAL CHASTITY

I'm including this amazing nugget of knowledge and wisdom because emotional chastity is a major supplement to your chastity exercise routine. I was so busy fighting for physical freedom that emotional chastity never even crossed my mind at the time. It's okay if you are focused on that like I was. This may be a section you don't visit or focus on until after you have made it further down the line, but I wanted to include it for when the time is right. God says, "Above all else, guard your heart, for everything flows from it." We get so busy protecting our bodies that we don't protect the most important thing of all, our hearts. Trying to disconnect our bodies from our hearts with sexual acts is anything but wise. The truth is, whether we realize it or not, the two are connected and the body very often follows the heart or its desires. Emotional chastity is not giving away your heart to anyone but your future spouse, same as our body. The two go together as a gift to our husband or wife.

So the question is how do we date as singles and simultaneously protect our hearts? The answer is: courting. Courting sets up dating situations so that you are less inclined to get attached prior to that major commitment. Group settings for dates are perfect. Family involvement for dates as well are wise because it's always helpful to have the people who want what's best for you give their blessing or concerns. Staying in public is another great option because you aren't in each other's personal, private spaces. All of these help you to be emotionally chaste, which contributes to chastity overall.

I also want to include in this something that is only talked about in Catholic circles, and that is a "near occasion of sin." This plays into emotional chastity because if you are just cuddling with someone, that may not be emotionally chaste and can lead to loss of your heart that only should go to your future spouse. It also can lead to losing your physical chastity in some instances. "Netflix and chill" could be a near occasion of sin for some and again can lead you to physically sinning. If one or both partners are not strong in that area, it's wise to not set up a situation that would be a temptation or a fall for you. Proverbs 4:7 says, "The beginning of wisdom is this: Get wisdom." If you are never alone in each other's cars or houses, that is a near occasion of sin that is removed. The temptation then is not even there for you to have to battle. The same goes for kissing, in my opinion. Passionate kissing (more than a peck) can definitely be problematic both emotionally and physically. There is a biblical quote that says, "Can a man scoop fire into his lap without his clothes being burned?" (Prv 6:27). In other words, don't start what you shouldn't finish. Would your kisses not have that effect? It is wise and chaste to not even start something you aren't planning on finishing.

MODESTY

Why is the modesty section being put in the chapter of all things Catholic? Supplements are by definition "a substance taken to remedy the deficiencies in a person's diet." Modesty helps to remedy any deficiencies in other people's purity. So you actually become a multivitamin supplement in holiness for them.

I won't go into too much detail on modesty because I think there are already amazing experts talking on this subject. Theology of the Body Institute is great with the "why," and I am especially fond of Jason and Crystalina Evert. My favorite on the subject, Leah Darrow, is also a great resource to check out. They have all you need, so I will only share my own experience with this.

Modesty, for me, was the very last step of my chastity and purity. It took a long time. It developed and improved over time. However, I will admit it's a very difficult thing to practice in our society. Even in our church, the definition of modesty seems to have quite a range. I do quite well at this point with my regular clothes, but it took many years of struggle with gym and workout clothes in Florida heat. It took forever, but I finally figured it out. I realized the best thing is to pray about each outfit before I leave the house and ask the Holy Spirit to convict me if I need to change anything. The second thing that works is putting a little skirt over your workout pants or shorts. *What I noticed overall is long after sexual sin is gone, you can still dress inappropriately out of pride or insecurity. Even when it's not sexual at all to you, it could tempt someone who is struggling.*

Modest dress is a balancing act. It's something that we don't want to get scrupulous about and basically put a bag on that covers us from head to toe because we are afraid someone will stumble from our outfits. At the same time, it's so imperative to be aware of our beauty (both men and women) and use that awareness in our wardrobe choices.

CONCLUSION

Ultimately, the Catholic Church was instituted by Christ and equipped by him to bring grace to a fallen world through the sacraments, sacramentals, and so many other beautiful devotional practices. All it has to offer is far too vast, far too big a call to holiness and continued spiritual growth for a lifetime to be compared to anything. It's been standing for thousands of years through everything the enemy has done to it and is doing to it today, trying to rip it apart from the inside out. And yet, it will stand till the end. Living a fully Catholic life has, without a doubt, given me the supernatural ability and strength to not only overcome but to be a gold medalist in Christ's gift of chastity.

The further you get away from the past when you were in prison, the more you can see clearly about all that was. While I could not have written now what I wrote three years ago, I would never have been ready then to write for you what I have now included in this chapter. I'm simply not the same person I was then, and now I am a continued testimony to the deepening and maturity of faith that occurs if you keep walking with the Lord, and how far you move when you escape from the bondage of sexual sin. They are memories of a past life I want to fade, a past life I tried so hard to get rid of, a past life I spent so long fighting tooth and nail to leave behind me. The more we try to leave those demons, the more they fight to hold onto us. However, they are also memories of God's grace for me, his mercy, his power, and his absolute miraculous answer to my prayers.

All of it changes a person in so many ways—the trying to break free and then the realization of that freedom, all the lakes of tears, and then all the tears of rejoicing when God finally answers (or when we finally answer him so he can do the miracle in our lives we begged from him). The fact that I'm different gives me a different mindset and perspective. Today, I wouldn't even compare this book to working out, I would compare all the how-tos within this text to instructions on being able to breathe; in other words, to life itself.

It has become such an intricate part of myself, it's almost second nature. It's not something I do, it's something that is. It is something that I am.

In final honor of this beautiful love for the Catholic Church that God put on my heart, I thought I would add a few additional days of devotional. It is my prayer that if you are not Catholic, you consider all the tools the Church offers to help you in your healing journey, and if you are Catholic, that you utilize those tools more and more in your walk with Christ.

FULLNESS DAY 1: THE EUCHARIST

"Then Jesus declared, 'I am the bread of life. Whoever comes to me will never go hungry and whoever believes in me will never be thirsty'" (Jn 6:35).

The precious Body and Blood of my Son, Jesus Christ, is what will make you whole. The more you are able to unite with us in this way, the more strength you will have to lead a life of holiness. How will you approach me, knowing that I am the Lord your God, who suffered, died, and was buried to save you? How often will you come to me, knowing that you have access to me in the Eucharist every day. Will you leave me alone in what was once mere bread and wine and is now transformed into my precious Blood and Body? Are you too busy to come to unite with me? I am the all-powerful, all-living God, and my freedom remains in this sacrament. Come, eat, drink, overcome all your sins through me as I am in you.

Prayer

Help me, Lord, to join with you more fully in this sacrament of holy Mass. There is nothing you can't do for me, if I let you. Why do I stay away? Why would I think for a minute anything is more important in my day than becoming one with you? I love you too much to stay away. Help me to find Mass times that I can be with you as many days a week as possible. Make a way Lord, so I can be free of these sins of the flesh. With you, nothing is impossible.

FULLNESS DAY 2: SACRAMENT OF RECONCILIATION

"'Which is easier: to say to this paralyzed man, "Your sins are forgiven," or to say, "Get up, take your mat and walk?" But I want you to know that the Son of Man has authority on earth to forgive sins.' So he said to the man, 'I tell you, get up, take your mat and go home'" (Mk 2:9–11).

I love you more than you can imagine. You wonder how that is possible and how you could be forgiven, but when you make a good act of contrition, when you show your love for our relationship and ask purely for forgiveness in the sacrament of Reconciliation, it is given to you. Please accept that forgiveness. Please let it go. When you are forgiven, you are forgiven. There is no need for you to stay sitting, paralyzed on your mat, when you have already been given the ability to walk again. And I don't only want you to walk, I'm showing you now how to run.

Prayer

Lord, with all those bad things that I did, it's so hard for me to believe that you really have forgiven me. So many mistakes and so many bad decisions led me far from you, but I want to be free so that I can walk and then run to you. Show me how. Help me let the past go and walk into this new season of freedom with you.

FULLNESS DAY 3: OUR LADY

"And no one pours new wine into old wineskins. Otherwise, the wine will burst the skins, and both the wine and the wineskins will be ruined. No, they pour new wine into new wineskins" (Mk 2:22).

It is time to walk with me into the promised land, free from shame and guilt. Let the past go. I was with you for all your days in the wilderness, and now I will be with you in a new land but you cannot take your past where I'm taking you. It will be preserved in your testimony, but you have to let it go. I have forgiven you and you must forgive yourself. Release yourself, so I am able to release you.

Prayer

I don't want to beat myself up any more about this. Through the intercession of Our Lady of Perpetual Help, my mother, comfort me as only a mother knows how. Help me prepare for where your son is taking me, Mary! I want to go with him.

BONUS: MEDIA DEVOTION

"Finally, brothers and sisters, whatever is true, whatever is noble, whatever is right, whatever is pure, whatever is lovely, whatever is admirable—if anything is excellent or praiseworthy—think about such things" (Phil 4:8).

Your mind that I gave you is one of pure and beautiful things. Remember back to when the thoughts you had were pure and beautiful, as a small child. I still want you to be childlike (not childish) in that awestruck wonder of innocent things. What are you watching? What are you listening to? Does it reflect me and that beauty? Or does it reflect and meditate on darkness? The things you take in to think about are the things that will pervade your mind. I have given you free will to choose those things. Will you choose me, or will you constantly choose perverse options the world and the evil one tempts you with? I have given you every tool, every grace, to strengthen you so that you may choose the good and pure and holy.

Prayer

Jesus, make me an instrument of your holiness. Give me the strength to renew my mind by only watching and listening to things that don't offend you or your Blessed Mother. When exposed to other people's conversations and movies and music and books, help me to discern and only take in what is of you, that which will bring me closer to you in heart, mind, and body.